The
Wisdom *of*
Solomon
and Us

The Quest for Meaning, Morality and a Deeper Relationship with God

Rabbi Marc D. Angel, PhD

For People of All Faiths, All Backgrounds

JEWISH LIGHTS Publishing

www.jewishlights.com

The Wisdom of Solomon and Us:
The Quest for Meaning, Morality and a Deeper Relationship with God

Library of Congress Cataloging-in-Publication Data
Names: Angel, Marc, author.
Title: The wisdom of Solomon and us : the quest for meaning, morality and a deeper relationship with God / Rabbi Marc D. Angel, PhD.
Description: Woodstock, VT : Jewish Lights Publishing, [2016] | Includes bibliographical references.
Identifiers: LCCN 2016011890| ISBN 9781580238557 (pbk.) | ISBN 9781580238601 (ebook)
Subjects: LCSH: Wisdom literature—Criticism, interpretation, etc. | Bible. Ecclesiastes—Criticism, interpretation, etc. | Bible. Proverbs—Criticism, interpretation, etc. | Bible. Song of Solomon—Criticism, interpretation, etc. | Solomon, King of Israel.
Classification: LCC BS1455 .A66 2016 | DDC 223/.06—dc23 LC record available at http://lccn.loc.gov/2016011890

ISBN-13: 978-1-68336-455-9 (hc)

Manufactured in the United States of America
Cover Design: Tim Holtz
Interior Design: Thor Goodrich
Cover Art: Shraga Weil, "Vanities of vanities...," S-144 Eccl VI, Safrai Gallery, Jerusalem, Israel; www.safrai.com
For People of All Faiths, All Backgrounds
Published by Jewish Lights Publishing
An Imprint of Turner Publishing Company
4507 Charlotte Avenue, Suite 100
Nashville, TN 37209
Tel: (615) 255-2665
www.jewishlights.com

Contents

PART TWO
Wisdom, Morality, and Righteousness– Proverbs/*Mishlei*

PART THREE
The Quest for Relationship with God– The Song of Songs/*Shir ha-Shirim*

Introduction

Toward the end of his novel, *Moby Dick*, Herman Melville includes a seemingly innocuous scene. But it is not innocuous.

Captain Ahab is obsessed with killing the great white whale Moby Dick. His ship is scouring the seas to locate his nemesis. Suddenly, the whale is sighted in the distance. Ahab is in a frenzy. The ship turns in the direction of the whale, but in the process Pip, the cabin boy, falls overboard.

A dilemma arises. If the ship stops to retrieve Pip, the whale may get away. Yet, if the ship does not stop to save Pip, the cabin boy may be lost. Ahab decides: we will pursue the whale, we can't let it escape. Once we kill Moby Dick, we can return and retrieve Pip.

So Pip is left to founder in the sea as the ship moves off in the direction of the whale. As the ship passes out of Pip's line of vision, the cabin boy finds himself in cosmic loneliness. In all directions, all he can see is the endless ocean. Above is the infinitely distant sky. Below is the cold darkness of the sea's depths. Pip is absolutely alone, without moorings, without anything to grasp onto.

Ahab's ship does indeed return to fetch Pip after its unsuccessful attempt to catch Moby Dick. But when Pip is pulled on board, he is now a very different person. Pip has lost his mind.

Melville was writing in the mid-nineteenth century, when more and more people were feeling like Pip. The old foundations of life were coming undone. Industrialization, scientific advances, significant demographic changes—these and other factors contributed to feelings of being alone in a vast and impersonal universe. But without moorings, one risked partial or total insanity.

In his poem "The Grande Chartreuse," Matthew Arnold, the great nineteenth-century English literary figure, described the feeling of "wandering between two worlds, one dead, / the other powerless to be born, / with nowhere yet to rest my head." People were losing the old intellectual and spiritual foundations of life but did not know exactly how to replace these foundations.

The dilemma of Pip in the nineteenth century became even more pronounced during the twentieth century and into the twenty-first century. The inexorable advances in science and technology have been accompanied by a parallel weakening of traditional religious beliefs and observances. For many, the theory of evolution undermines the biblical understanding of humans having been created in the image of God. The "uncertainty principle," which has become a mainstay of modern physics, is also a characteristic of modern life in many areas. People are uncertain of the truths that they have inherited. There is a "new morality," a "new relativism," a "new me-centeredness," and— among many individuals—a new angst.

In his book *Man's Search for Meaning*, the eminent psychiatrist Viktor Frankl writes of the existential vacuum that has taken hold among the new generations. People wonder: Does my life have any ultimate meaning? Is human existence simply the result of blind chance? Am I just a random atom occupying an infinitesimally small bit of time and space, here by accident and soon to vanish without trace? Lacking meaningful answers to these questions, a person feels a spiritual vacuum, an emptiness within.

Dr. Peter Berger, an insightful analyst of contemporary religious life, has described the modern period as one of spiritual homelessness. In their book *The Homeless Mind*, he and his coauthor H. Kellner note that many thoughtful people have become—or are becoming—alienated from traditional religious teachings and rites that had served as major social anchors for the earlier generations. They have sought answers to their life's questions in science or philosophy.

In confronting the modern and postmodern zeitgeist, some have sought to isolate themselves in physical and spiritual ghettos. They follow cultlike leaders who claim to have *the* truth. They pretend that nothing has changed, and they adhere to a fundamentalist traditionalism that often is antiscience, antimodernity, and anti-intellectual.

Others think that everything has changed. They toss away the religious and cultural baggage of the past. The new focus is on autonomy, personal freedom, and the right to choose whatever life-style one wishes, as long as it does not directly hurt someone else. If life has no ultimate meaning, why not simply "eat, drink, and be merry"?

Yet others seek to draw on the ideas and ideals of traditional religion, while applying these values to a new and different world. They seek to be anchored to eternal teachings but also to foster the values of individualism and personal freedom. They seek to create a way of life that is meaningful and intellectually sound; they try to purge their spiritual lives of superstition, obscurantism, and blind fundamentalism.

While Pip's existential dilemma seems to be so modern, questions of meaning have confronted human beings from the outset of human history. And just as various modern responses to spiritual restlessness are varied, so human beings throughout the ages have sought different answers to their ultimate questions.

The Wisdom of Solomon

The Bible describes King Solomon as having been granted the gift of wisdom by God. As the wisest of all people, Solomon's fame spread within his kingdom of Israel and throughout his part of the world. The Bible ascribes three books to Solomon's authorship: Ecclesiastes (*Koheleth*), Proverbs (*Mishlei*), and the Song of Songs (*Shir ha-Shirim*). If these biblical books are attributed to Solomon and Solomon was the wisest of all people, then these books deserve to be studied carefully. What can we moderns learn from this wise ancient king of Israel?

These three biblical books have very different tones and styles. Ecclesiastes is a philosophical text, struggling to find meaning in life. Proverbs is a collection of pithy statements extolling the virtues of wisdom, morality, and faith in God. The Song of Songs is a lyrical love poem.

Sages of the Midrash—ancient Rabbinic lore of Talmudic times—suggested that Solomon wrote these books at different stages of his life. When he was young and amorous, he wrote love poetry—the Song of Songs. As he grew older, he mellowed and became concerned about wisdom and ethics; so in his maturity, he wrote Proverbs. As he grew old, he became more cynical. In spite of the fact that he had lived with all the luxuries of a wise and powerful king, he wondered if life had any ultimate meaning. In this questioning and despondent mood, he wrote *Koheleth*, lamenting the vanity and emptiness of life.

Rabbi Moshe Almosnino, a leading rabbi of sixteenth-century Salonika, wrote commentaries on these books (*Yedei Moshe*).[1] In the introduction to this work, he offered—and preferred—a different ordering of Solomon's books based on the writings of kabbalists. According to this view, Solomon wrote his philosophical speculations, Ecclesiastes, as a young man in search of truth and meaning in life. As he entered middle age, he turned his thoughts to running his kingdom in a way that promoted righteousness and goodness among the people of his nation. This led him to write Proverbs. But as he grew old, he took a profound spiritual turn; as an old man, he wrote the Song of Songs as a love poem that exuded the human yearning for love of God. Thus Solomon evolved from the philosophical, to the moralistic, to the spiritual.

In support of this view, Rabbi Almosnino cites the superscriptions that open each of the three works. Ecclesiastes begins, "The words of Koheleth, the son of David, king in Jerusalem." Solomon presents himself in an apologetic, defensive tone. He is a young man, somewhat unsure of himself. He wants readers to pay heed to his book, but he is reluctant even to give his own name. He writes with the pen name Koheleth, "the one who teaches in assemblies" (from the Hebrew word *kahal*, "community"). To bolster his credentials, he identifies himself as the son of the great King David. Solomon identifies himself humbly as king in Jerusalem, rather than as king over all Israel.

In contrast, the book of Proverbs opens, "The proverbs of Solomon the son of David, king of Israel." Here, Solomon is writing at full strength, with confidence and authority. He identifies himself by name and as king of Israel. He refers to his illustrious father, David, famed king whose reputation was well known to his audience. With this superscription, Solomon is demanding the attention of his readers. He is a great king, with great lineage.

The Song of Songs opens, "The Song of Songs, which is Solomon's." At this late stage in his life, Solomon has reached a new spiritual plateau. He does not need to impress anyone with his title or with his descent from King David. He is simply Solomon. In the eyes of God, it is ludicrous to puff oneself up with titles and lineage: each person stands alone in the presence of God.

According to this view, then, Solomon first wrote Ecclesiastes while he was a young man, lacking full confidence and plagued by uncertainty. As he matured and reached his status as wise king of Israel, he shared his wisdom by writing Proverbs. But then, as an old man, he outgrew his earlier stages of life and came to see himself as one person seeking a loving relationship with the Almighty. His title, wealth, and reputation were of little concern at this point in his spiritual development.

In this book, I follow the interpretation favored by Rabbi Almosnino. Drawing on passages within each of Solomon's books, I offer musings on how this ancient wisdom may be viewed through the eyes of moderns.

The first section of the book is based on Ecclesiastes and deals with such issues as the quest for meaning in life; faith and doubt; divine justice.

The second section is based on the book of Proverbs and deals with such topics as righteousness, wisdom, the good life, morality.

The third section is based on the Song of Songs and deals with the human quest for spirituality, relationship with the Almighty, love of God, personal transcendence through love.

This book is not a commentary on these biblical books, nor is it an academic biblical study. Its starting point is the framework given by ancient Rabbinic tradition to these works—that all were composed by King Solomon, the wisest of all people. While historians and Bible scholars will have their own views on the nature of these works, I am setting this book squarely within the framework of Rabbinic tradition. Ecclesiastes, Proverbs, and the Song of Songs were intended to be expressions of profound wisdom that could be helpful and meaningful to all future generations. These books are classic representatives of ancient Israel's Wisdom Literature.

Ecclesiastes (*Koheleth*)

The Talmud (*Shabbat* 30b) raises the question, why was Ecclesiastes included in the Hebrew Bible? The book is filled with doubts and with seemingly heretical ideas. Even granting that it was written by King Solomon, why would such a work be included in the biblical canon, as one of the divinely sanctioned texts? The suggested answer was that the book opens with piety and ends with piety. In spite of its problematic features, its basic premise is that one should fear the Almighty and observe God's commandments, for that is the greatest attainment available to human beings.

Rabbi Hayyim Angel, in an essay on Ecclesiastes, notes that while the prophetic works of the Bible record God's messages to human beings, Ecclesiastes is among those biblical texts that reflect the musings of a human being, not messages conveyed by God to the author.[2] The Rabbinic sages who decided to include Ecclesiastes in the Bible were making a tremendously important statement: honest questioning is a legitimate aspect of religious life. It was an act of religious genius to canonize Ecclesiastes and thereby to recognize and sanction the doubts of sincere religious seekers. Instead of banning such thoughts, instead of pretending that blind faith is enough, the sages made Ecclesiastes an integral part of our religious adventure.

Proverbs (*Mishlei*)

Solomon's wisdom found expression in proverbs. He utilized short, pithy statements to underscore basic themes in his religious outlook. Unlike the complex and sometimes anguished verses in Ecclesiastes, the verses in Proverbs are relatively straightforward and uncomplicated.

The Talmudic sages wondered whether Proverbs was simply a reflection of Solomon's human wisdom or whether it was divinely inspired. They found a number of proverbs that seemed to be contradictory or otherwise problematic. Nevertheless, they concluded that Proverbs did reflect divine authorization. The proverbs were composed by Solomon with a mind that was attuned to the spirit of God.

The Song of Songs (*Shir ha-Shirim*)

The Song of Songs is a lyrical love poem portraying the passions of a young maiden and her beloved. It has been variously interpreted as a love story between the maiden and the king; or between the maiden and a shepherd, but with the king interested in winning over the maiden; or as a collection of love poems without a particular story line.

Why is the Song of Songs included in the Bible? It seems to have nothing to do with God or with religious teaching. The Talmudic Rabbis mulled over the sanctity—or lack thereof—of this love poem, but Rabbi Akiva put the issue to rest once and for all. He stated (*Mishnah Yadayim* 3:5), "All the world is not worthy as the day on which the Song of Songs was given to Israel, for all the *Ketuvim* [Writings] are holy, but the Song of Songs is the Holy of Holies."

Rabbi Akiva saw in the Song of Songs the spiritual longing and love that tied God and the people of Israel together. Solomon employed love symbolism as a parable of the love between God and Israel.

Poets and mystics of subsequent generations followed Rabbi Akiva's approach, drawing great spiritual energy from the Song of Songs and viewing it as a sacred rather than a secular text. They saw it as a parable not only of love between God and Israel, but the love between a human being and God.

Who Was Solomon?

Solomon inherited the throne of Israel from his father David. His reign is generally thought to have been approximately from 970 to 930 BCE. When he first assumed the throne, he was still a young man. The first book of Kings describes his initial acquisition of wisdom:

> In Gibeon the Lord appeared to Solomon in a dream by night; and God said, "Ask what I shall give you." And Solomon said, "... You have made Your servant king instead of David my father; and I am but a little child; I know not how to go out or come in. And Your servant is in the midst of the people that You have chosen, a great

people, that cannot be numbered nor counted for multitude. Give therefore to Your servant an understanding
heart to judge Your people, that I may discern between
good and bad; for who is able to judge this so great a
people?" (1 Kings 3:5–9).

In response to Solomon's request, God replied, "Since you have
asked for this and not for long life or wealth for yourself, nor have
asked for the death of your enemies but for discernment in admin-
istering justice, I will do what you have asked" (1 Kings 3:11–12).
The Bible notes, "The whole world sought audience with Solomon
to hear the wisdom God had put in his heart" (1 Kings 10:24).

During Solomon's reign, the Temple in Jerusalem was constructed, and impressive building projects were launched throughout
the country. Israel was strong and prosperous. The Bible informs us
that Solomon married numerous wives, including many from idolatrous nations. He allowed these wives to worship their idols, and he is
severely criticized in the Bible for his tolerance of—and participation
in—idolatrous worship. So although he was the wisest of kings, he
also had flaws of character. His very imperfections, though, make him
a more realistic personality. He was not a plaster saint but a flesh and
blood human being—very much like the rest of humanity.

As we relate to texts reflective of Solomon's spiritual journey, we
will find that his wisdom has continued to resonate through the
generations. It speaks to us.

A Note on the Texts

The English translations of the biblical texts are drawn from *The
Holy Scriptures*, issued by the Jewish Publication Society, Philadelphia, 1979; *The Five Megilloth*, Soncino Press, London, 1967; and
Proverbs, Soncino Press, London, 1967. I have made some minor
modifications to these translations.

Throughout this book, following biblical style, I refer to God in
the masculine form. God, of course, is neither masculine nor femi-
nine; whatever pronouns or adjectives we use in relation to the
Almighty are all to be understood as symbolic, not literal.

PART ONE

The Quest for Meaning

Ecclesiastes/*Koheleth*

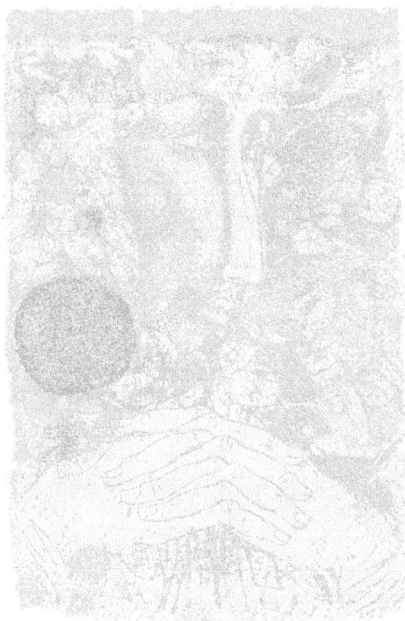

The Cosmic and
the Human Perspectives

The words of Koheleth, the son of David, king in Jerusalem. Vanity of vanities, says Koheleth; vanity of vanities,
all is vanity. What profit has man of all his labor wherein
he labors under the sun?

(ECCLESIASTES 1:1–3)

The Talmud (*Hagigah* 14b) reports that four great sages entered
the *pardes*, the domain of mystical speculation: Ben Azzai, Ben
Zoma, Rabbi Elisha ben Avuya, and Rabbi Akiva. They wanted to
find ultimate truth about God, about the meaning of human life,
about the mysteries that elude human understanding. Their experi-
ment led to tragic results.

As they began their voyage in the *pardes*, Rabbi Akiva warned his
colleagues, "When you reach the domain of pure marble, don't call
out 'water, water'; as it is written (Psalm 101:7), 'One who speaks
falsehoods will not be established before My eyes.'" Rabbi Akiva
reminded them how easy it is to mistake clear marble for water, a
metaphor for the common inability to distinguish between truth
and falsehood. People are prone to follow external appearances
rather than search for the hidden meanings that lay beneath and
beyond the surface realities.

In spite of his warnings, the three colleagues of Rabbi Akiva did
not fare well. Ben Azzai was overwhelmed by the experience and he
died. Ben Zoma became so confused and mentally unsettled that he
lost his mind. Elisha ben Avuya became a heretic and was thereafter
known in Talmudic literature as *Aher*, "the other one." Only Rabbi
Akiva entered the *pardes* in peace and exited it in peace.

The Talmud notes the root of Rabbi Elisha ben Avuya's heresy. He concluded that there is no justice and no Judge. The more he attempted to understand the secrets of God and the meaning of human life, the more convinced he became that everything is random. Society did not seem to be governed by a Righteous Divinity that rewarded the just and punished the wicked. Things just happened.

Rabbi Akiva emerged from the *pardes* in peace. The Talmud does not record what great wisdom he had discovered, nor why he had been successful while his colleagues had failed.

I understand this story to be teaching that all four of the sages were tormented by the same questions and uncertainties. But only Rabbi Akiva found a way to live without having clear answers. The questions were powerful enough to unhinge the three others, but Rabbi Akiva was able to live with unanswered questions.

Many years ago I wrote a story (unpublished) about a debate between the greatest theologian and the greatest atheist. Did God create the world, or is the universe the result of random processes? Both of them entered a time capsule that was to be plummeted back to the beginning of time. They would see with their own eyes how the universe began. Once they both witnessed the origin of the cosmos, they would know one way or the other if God created it or if it just happened on its own. As their time capsule approached the first moments of the universe, it shook wildly, tossing the two men to and fro. For an instant, they witnessed the first moment of the universe, and then the time capsule returned them to the present.

When they emerged, the atheist announced, "I was wrong. There surely is a God, Creator of the universe. I saw God with my own eyes." The theologian announced, "I was wrong. There is no God. The big bang just happened by itself."

Human beings may look at the same data and come to different conclusions. Rabbi Elisha ben Avuya could not solve the riddle of life, so he concluded that there simply was no riddle! Life is random, without metaphysical meaning. Rabbi Akiva understood that there were deeper truths beyond the evidence that meets the eyes. He was able to perceive that marble was not water.

The four sages who entered the *pardes*, like all inquiring human beings, could not find absolute answers to their questions. Perhaps Rabbi Akiva's genius was not only the ability to live with questions, but the wisdom to frame the questions in a different way.

From the cosmic perspective, human life certainly seems like vanity and striving after wind. In the face of eternity, what is the significance of the infinitesimal span of our lives? In relation to the billions of stars and countless galaxies, what is the meaning of our tiny existence on the planet earth? The Psalmist was aware of the cosmic perspective: "When I behold Your heavens, the work of Your fingers, the moon and the stars which You have established; what is man that You are mindful of him, and the son of man that You think of him?" (Psalm 8:4–5).Compared to the vastness of time and space, we literally seem to be nothing, of no consequence. If we live or die, the universe continues on its own course as though we had never existed.

However, the Psalmist then adds another perspective: "But You have made him but little lower than the angels and have crowned him with glory and honor" (Psalm 8:6). Yes, we seem to be nothing compared to the nameless and faceless cosmos, but we are something in relation to God! Our lives are imbued with meaning because God created us and because we are, in some mysterious way, part of God's plan. Our lives matter.

Rabbi Elisha ben Avuya stopped at the cosmic perspective. Rabbi Akiva penetrated to the human perspective. Rabbi Elisha found a cold, material, and random universe in which human life makes no sense. Rabbi Akiva found a life filled with spiritual value and meaning.

Ecclesiastes, perhaps the most human book of the Bible, begins with the cosmic perspective. Solomon looks around as objectively as he can, and he sees the futility and senselessness of human life. *Hevel havalim*, "vanity of vanities"! *Hevel* literally means "breath, wind." Life passes like a breeze; it is insubstantial, impermanent. It disappears without leaving a trace.

But although breath is insubstantial and transient, we could not live without it!

Confronting Our Mortality

One generation passes away and another generation comes; and the earth abides forever. The sun also rises, and the sun goes down, and hastens to its place where it arises.

(ECCLESIASTES 1:4–5)

Visit any cemetery, especially an old historic cemetery, and you will see the tombstones of human beings who lived and died and who left hardly a dent in the fabric of time and space. Generations disappear, new generations arise, and they too disappear, making way for yet other new generations. And those generations inevitably also will disappear. The tombstones are an attempt to give some permanence to the life of the person buried underneath, and yet the tombstones eventually crumble and fade with the passage of time.

Does any of this make sense? Does any human life really matter in the overall scheme of things? We toil and struggle to make our way through life, only to die, and soon to be forgotten. And even if we are remembered, it is only for a relatively short time. And even if we are remembered for a few thousand years, what difference does it make? Those who remember us are also frail mortals who will pass away soon enough. If we think of the eternity of time and the vastness of space, what significance can there be to a life that extends even for a few thousand years?

A generation comes and a generation goes, and the earth abides forever. Yes, that is true from the cosmic perspective.

But from the human perspective, the death of a loved one is an overwhelming experience. The passing of a parent or grandparent, and the passing of a generation, mean a great deal to us from our vantage point.

When a parent or grandparent dies, we sense the universal truth that all living beings die, that all humans are mortal. We understand this on a philosophical level, and we even may feel wise in doing so. Yet, we also understand that something unsettling has happened, that there is something new under the sun as far as we are concerned. In the face of the death of a loved one, our philosophical wisdom becomes shockingly inadequate. A parent dies, and we cry. The death seems like something new and unique, as though no one else had died in the past.

When a generation passes on, the lives of the surviving generations are altered. As long as we had the elders with us, we also had access to their stories, their experiences. They were living links with our own past, and they helped us understand the context of our lives. We enjoyed hearing about their childhoods and their memories of family members who had passed on long ago.

The Israeli poet Amnon Shamosh had left Syria as a youth to live on a kibbutz in Israel. In his poem "The Great Confession," he describes how each summer his mother would visit him and fill his ears with stories and traditions. As a young man, he paid little attention to his mother's memories. She was "the old world," and he was living in a new time and a new place. One summer, his mother did not come on her annual visit. She had died. Shamosh suddenly found himself wanting to hear his mother's stories and to recapture every detail. But there were so many things he didn't remember; now that his mother had died, he could no longer ask her for information. "I wanted to hear her tell more and more / but my mother who came to me each summer / (across the barrier) / had been— and gone."[1]

When a parent dies, a source of our civilization dies; we are cut off; we are amazed by how many things we wanted to ask but never got around to asking, by how many things we heard but did not pay careful enough attention. Our past seems to shrink or to freeze.

When my mother, Rachel Romey Angel, died in May 1983, I officiated at her funeral. During my eulogy, I spontaneously said, "Now I am an orphan. My brothers and sister are orphans." Even as I uttered those words, I felt that they were strange. The word "orphan" implies vulnerability and even a sense of helplessness. Yet I, my brothers, and my sister were all married with families of our own. We were not helpless but were in the middle of our own lives. Nonetheless, I felt that we were orphaned with the passing of my mother in 1983 and then orphaned completely with the passing of my father, Victor B. Angel, in the summer of 1991. The death of a parent changes our life in practical and abstract ways; we never stop missing a deceased parent, and the parent never ceases to be part of the lives of children and grandchildren. (See my book *The Orphaned Adult*.)[2]

The novelist Peter De Vries in his book *Let Me Count the Ways* observes, "That you can't go home again is a truth inseparably linked to the fact that neither can you ever get away from it."[3] Children grow up, become independent, and leave their childhood homes behind. Good parents encourage this process, even if there is a poignant melancholy in watching children move away and go on with their lives. Yet, no one ever fully gets away from the parents' home. The memories and values, the experiences and adventures of childhood, form the foundation of our personalities. Although we become adults, we never stop being children. Although we are the next generation, we are inextricably linked to the past generation. And we know that our time on earth will also come to an end; we want to leave values, and meaning, and happiness to our next generations.

From the vantage point of the cosmos, one life or one generation or all human history do not amount to very much. But from our human vantage point, one life and one generation and all human history tell us who we are. We are not Pip flailing around in the ocean.

Creativity and Wonder

All the rivers run into the sea, yet the sea is not full; to the place where the rivers go, so they go again.... That which has been is that which shall be. And that which has been done is that which shall be done; and there is nothing new under the sun. Is there a thing whereof it is said: "See, this is new?" It has been already in the ages that were before us.

(ECCLESIASTES 1:7, 1:9–10)

When Albert Einstein was a little boy, his father showed him a compass. The needle pointed north no matter which way Einstein turned the compass around. The child was amazed. In his autobiography published in 1949, Einstein recalls his feelings on that occasion:

> The needle behaved in such a determined way and did not fit into the usual explanation of how the world works. That is that you must touch something to move it. I still remember now, or I believe that I remember, that this experience made a deep and lasting impression on me. There must be something deeply hidden behind everything.[1]

But more than his amazement about the compass, Einstein gained another insight: "Why do we come, sometimes spontaneously, to wonder about something? I think that wondering to one's self occurs when an experience conflicts with our fixed ways of seeing the world."[2]

When we are jarred from complacency, when we are challenged to think in new ways, we become open to new insights. Intellectual

9

friction is fructifying. It makes us rethink old assumptions; it drives us to think along new pathways. While the rhythms of nature follow their fixed patterns, and while human civilization has much in it that seems highly repetitive or inevitable, each human being does, in fact, have the capacity to see things in a new light. Indeed, innovation and creativity are hallmarks of human life at its best.

Writing in ancient times, the wise King Solomon could not envision the explosion of knowledge in subsequent eras, and very especially in the past few centuries of the modern period. There may be nothing new under the sun, but humans have surely come up with new ideas, new technologies, and new ways of organizing life. The laws of nature may always have been in place, but our understanding of these laws has entailed centuries of research, experimentation, imagination, and innovative thinking. King Solomon might have modified his words if he had been aware of relativity, quantum mechanics, nuclear physics, DNA, modern technology, and so many other new developments.

Advances in human civilization have been the result of creativity and a sense of wonder. Although the natural world is fixed and unchanging, each individual human being is an original organism. If we go through life thinking that nothing can change and that we are destined to follow the paths of our predecessors, then it is unlikely that we will be able to break through the stagnation and boredom of being in a rut. But if we are open to new ideas and new challenges, we can experience life as a tremendous adventure.

Many of the best, most creative, and most dynamic leaders and thinkers have achieved greatness precisely because of spiritual and intellectual conflict. They have had to evaluate and reevaluate their assumptions; this process has strengthened them and helped them to open new pathways of thought and spirit.

The Talmud (*Bava Metzia* 84a) relates how Rabbi Yohanan deeply mourned the passing of his beloved colleague Reish Lakish. The Rabbis wanted to assuage Rabbi Yohanan's grief, and they assigned Rabbi Eleazar ben Pedath to go and study Torah with him. After each statement of Rabbi Yohanan, Rabbi Eleazar cited a proof in support. Instead of consoling Rabbi Yohanan, this deepened his sadness. "When I stated a law, the son of Lakish used to raise twenty-four objections, to which I gave twenty-four answers, and this consequently led to a fuller understanding of the law." He chastised Rabbi Eleazar for being a yes-man. Proper study entails sharp questions, critical thinking, and a lively give-and-take.

In *Pirkei Avot* 2:19, we find the opinion of Rabbi Elazar: "Be alert to learn Torah; know what to answer an unbeliever." Alertness implies having an agile mind, not only mastering texts but demonstrating eagerness to explore new ideas and interpretations. When Rabbi Elazar advises that one must know what to answer an unbeliever, he is warning against obscurantism and authoritarianism. He is calling on us to be aware of the critiques of others in a serious way. Through the analysis of the critiques, we are forced to think through the issues more carefully, not simply to accept past assumptions blindly.

Many seem to think that being religious is exemplified by shutting out conflicts and challenges from the surrounding civilization. For religion at its best, though, the opposite is the case. It is precisely by facing conflicts and challenges in a serious way that our religious life becomes stronger, more dynamic, and more creative. Our founding personalities like Abraham, Joseph, and Moses demonstrate the truth of this approach. So do the many great leaders and thinkers over the generations who have courageously and honestly faced the intellectual and spiritual challenges of their times and places.

Albert Einstein thought that "there must be something deeply hidden behind everything." This insight applies to a religious worldview as well as to science. If we are alert and maintain an open and eager mind, we may well discover the deep meanings hidden within. And we will discover new thoughts and new insights, thereby demonstrating that there are new things under the sun ... a lot of new things.

Humility: The Root of Wisdom

I Koheleth have been king over Israel in Jerusalem. And I applied my heart to seek and to search out by wisdom concerning all things that are done under heaven; it is a sore task that God has given to humans to be exercised therewith. I have seen all the works that are done under the sun; and behold, all is vanity and a striving after wind.

(ECCLESIASTES 1:12–14)

When I was a graduate student at Yeshiva University, I often did research in the remarkable Jewish Division of the New York Public Library on Forty-Second Street and Fifth Avenue. On one occasion, the librarian let me enter the stacks area where the vast collection of publications is kept. It was an awesome experience to see shelf after shelf of books, journals, pamphlets, microfilms, and so on. At first I was elated to view the collection.

But then I became depressed!

I was an eager graduate student pursuing wisdom. I was young, confident, excited at the prospect of discovering knowledge and becoming a scholar. After having seen the seemingly endless rows of books in the Jewish Division stacks, I came to the stark realization that I would forever remain ignorant. There was simply too much knowledge to obtain. If I were to live a thousand years, I would not be able to read everything in those stacks, let alone remember all of the contents.

And that was only the Jewish Division. The library had so many other vast collections that had to be mastered. Not only could I never read and retain everything, but no one could.

The human mind is finite. The world of knowledge is infinite. No matter how much we know, there is an infinity that we do not know.

The morning prayers in the traditional Jewish prayer book include the following passage:

> What are we? What is our life? What is our goodness? What is our righteousness? What our help? What our strength? What our power? What can we say in Your presence, O Lord our God, God of our ancestors? Are not the mightiest as nothing before You, people of renown as if they were not, the wise as if without knowledge, the intelligent as if lacking in understanding? For our doings are often confusion, and the days of our life as vanity before You. Even the human excelling the beast is nothing, for all is vanity, except only the pure soul, which must hereafter give accounting before Your glorious throne.

We begin our day confronting the fundamental reality: compared to the infinite wisdom of God, all our wisdom amounts to exceedingly little. That honest assessment can certainly be depressing.

But while it is hopeless for us to attain all knowledge and all wisdom, the little that we can attain is not altogether worthless. While the prayer acknowledges the overwhelming limitations to our intellectual pursuits, it also acknowledges that we have a soul and that we will give an accounting of our lives before God. If our souls are answerable to God, then our lives mean something. Whatever wisdom we gain is not altogether worthless. Even if we cannot do more than scratch the surface, that scratch is a testament that we have lived.

Rabbi Aryeh Kaplan, one of the most remarkable Jewish thinkers of the twentieth century, maintained that our attainment of wisdom must first start with our sense of "nothingness." He pointed to a profound teaching of the kabbalists: the Hebrew word for "I" is *ani*; if the letters of this word are rearranged, the result is *ayin*, "nothing"! The implication is that the real "I" is the nothingness within me.[1]

In this vein, Rabbinic tradition interprets the biblical verse "And wisdom, where is it to be found [*ve-hahokhmah me-ayin timatzei*]?" (Job 28:12). The Hebrew words can be read to mean "And wisdom is to be found in nothingness." Unless we can plummet to the depths of our own internal nothingness, we cannot undertake the process of proper spiritual development. We cannot attain wisdom without first having the humility to know that we do not know.

The experience of the Greek philosopher Socrates echoes this insight. The oracle of Delphi declared that there was no man wiser than Socrates, but Socrates himself found this pronouncement to be very strange. In Plato's *Apology*, Socrates is described as searching for others who were indeed wiser than he. He went to politicians, to poets, to artisans; he went from person to person inquiring of their wisdom. In the end, though, he found that none of them could truly be called wise.

> And I am called wise, for my hearers always imagine that I myself possess the wisdom which I find wanting in others: but the truth is, O men of Athens, that God only is wise; and by his answer he intends to show that the wisdom of men is worth little or nothing; he is not speaking of Socrates, he is only using my name by way of illustration, as if he said "He, O men, is the wisest, who like Socrates, knows that his wisdom is in truth worth nothing."[2]

Humility is not only the first step to whatever genuine wisdom is available to human beings; humility is the only key we have. Without it, all is vanity and striving after wind.

Imperfect Humanity

That which is crooked cannot be made straight; and that which is wanting cannot be numbered.... For in much wisdom is much vexation; and one who increases knowledge increases sorrow.

(ECCLESIASTES 1:15, 1:18)

The erudite twentieth-century thinker Dr. Isaiah Berlin found much truth in this statement of Immanuel Kant: "Out of the crooked timber of humanity no straight thing was ever made." Humanity is by nature imperfect. We create various societies with differing ideas and values, each with its own strengths and weaknesses. We do not all look alike or think alike. When idealists or tyrants seek to homogenize humanity into one neat package, the result is not true to human nature.

Dr. Berlin argues that "to force people into the neat uniforms demanded by dogmatically believed-in schemes is almost always the road to inhumanity."[1] There is not one true answer to every question. There is not one true ideal of humanity or of an individual human being. To compel uniformity to an abstract ideal is to undermine the very fabric of humanity, which is by nature diverse, idiosyncratic, and imperfect. Our "crookedness" is a function of our individuality; to try to iron it out of us is to extinguish our individualism.

Yet, the "crookedness" is a fundamental problem of humanity. The more we study history, the more is our vexation with the imperfections of the human race. From time immemorial, human beings have been engaged in war and violence, in oppression of the weak, in plunder and theft, in hatred and bias against the "other." Is humanity any better today than it was in antiquity? We certainly

15

have achieved new levels of knowledge and technology, but we also have new powers of mass destruction, economic strangulation, and political injustice. We have wars in many regions, murders and other violent crimes in every country, billions of people who go to sleep hungry every night. It does sometimes seem that the more we know about humanity, the more sorrowful we become. But the problem is not only about humanity in general, but also about individual human beings.

A popular quip has it that "I love humanity; it's the people I don't like." It sometimes seems easier to love an abstract concept like humanity or the community rather than to love actual individuals. After all, human beings are not always pleasant or nice, courteous or considerate. Individuals can be rude, obnoxious, violent, and immoral. We can more easily love the abstract concept of humanity than deal with the negative features of particular individuals.

Dr. Robert Winters, who taught at Princeton University in the 1960s, offers a different perspective:

> When I look at the human race all over the world, I think there's zero reason for humanity to survive. We're destructive, uncaring, thoughtless, greedy, power hungry. But when I look at a few individuals, there seems every reason for humanity to survive.[2]

Humanity as a whole may be seriously flawed, but uniquely good and loving individuals make things worthwhile. Life takes on meaning not by focusing attention on humanity, but by appreciating particular human beings, outstanding individuals.

We can spend life being bitter over the imperfections of humanity and human beings; the crooked timber of humanity will never become entirely straight. Or we can focus on uniquely wonderful human beings and be grateful that they make life worthwhile. And perhaps most importantly, we can strive to become uniquely wonderful human beings who help justify humanity's existence.

The Rat Race

So I was great, and increased more than all that were
before me in Jerusalem; also my wisdom stood me in
stead. And whatsoever mine eyes desired I kept not from
them; I withheld not my heart from any joy, for my heart
had joy of all my labor; and this was my portion from all
my labor. Then I looked on all the works that my hands
had wrought, and on the labor that I had labored to do;
and behold, all was vanity and a striving after wind, and
there was no profit under the sun.

(ECCLESIASTES 2:9–11)

UBS Wealth Management Americas issued a report (April 28, 2015)
based on a survey of 2,215 U.S. investors with more than one million dollars net worth. It found that while these wealthy individuals
are pleased with their good fortune,

> they feel compelled to strive for more, spurred on by their
> own ambition, their desire to protect their families' life-
> style, and an ever-present fear of losing it all. As a result,
> many feel stuck on a treadmill, without a real sense of
> how much wealth would make them satisfied enough to
> get off.[1]

The majority of those interviewed felt that they achieved financial
success at the cost of losing precious time with family. Most felt that
their children ran the risk of being spoiled, of not really knowing
the value of money. And most felt the need to "keep up with the
Joneses," thereby increasing their expenditures in maintaining their
place in the rat race.

In his popular book *When All You've Ever Wanted Isn't Enough*, Rabbi Harold Kushner describes how people strive to attain certain goals, but when they achieve these goals, they are not necessarily happy. They have climbed the mountain and have an immediate sense of elation; but then they wonder what was gained by all that time and effort. Rabbi Kushner writes about people who have the outward trappings of success yet feel hollow inside:

> They can never rest and enjoy their accomplishments. They need one new success after another. They need constant reassurance from the people around them to still the voice inside them that keeps saying, "If other people knew you the way I know you, they would know what a phony you are."[2]

Dr. Barry Schwartz in his remarkable book *The Paradox of Choice* observes:

> We get what we say we want, only to discover that what we want doesn't satisfy us to the degree that we expect. We are surrounded by modern, time-saving devices, but we never seem to have enough time. We are free to be the authors of our own lives, but we don't know exactly what kind of lives we want to "write."[3]

When I was a student at Yeshiva College, I was once in the 181st Street IRT subway station and noted a sentence that had been scribbled onto one of the large advertisement posters on the wall of the subway platform. That sentence, by Alan Watts, had a profound impact on me then and still resonates strongly with me fifty years later: "For when a man no longer confuses himself with the definition of himself that others have given him, he is at once universal and unique."[4]

People are inauthentic when they strive to live according to the values and standards of others and in the process forfeit their own values and standards. They know in themselves that they want to live happy and meaningful lives, yet they find themselves drawn into a rat race in which they fear to fall behind. They compete; they see others as antagonists; they adopt external standards of success and want to live in a big house, drive an expensive car, be important, and have important friends. And when they have achieved these goals, they realize that the success is hollow. They've lost themselves in the process.

In his novel *Babbitt*, Sinclair Lewis describes a highly successful businessman who seems to have everything he could have wanted. Yet, Babbitt felt a tremendous lack within himself. He had a beautiful house with appropriate furnishings. Yes, he had a house ... but he felt he did not have a home. He was living someone else's life, someone else's dream.

If we spend our lives allowing others to define us, we will always feel a hollowness within, a sense of betraying our real selves. If we find that we are successful and yet feel that our lives are vanity and striving after wind, then we know—perhaps too late—that we've taken the wrong path.

Solomon was looking for meaning, but he was looking in the wrong places. He thought that his attainment of wealth, fame, and power would endow him with a sense of purpose in life. But these things were external to him, external to his inner being. They were signs of success that society imposed upon him, and they lured him away from his true self.

Looking Forward

The wise man, his eyes are in his head; but the fool walks in darkness.

(ECCLESIASTES 2:14)

My grandfather Marco Romey used to tell us—based on a kabbalistic teaching—that each person is placed on earth to fulfill a specific mission. Some people discover that mission and strive to accomplish it. Others spend a lifetime and never figure it out. And some do not even realize that they have a mission to fulfill!

Having "our eyes in our head" is essential for clarifying direction in life. We need to think clearly and see clearly, not get sidetracked by distractions. "Walking in darkness" means not knowing where we are going, not being able to decipher the way forward.

A wit once commented that people seek longevity even though they don't know what to do with themselves on a rainy Sunday afternoon. They fritter away their time with aimless pastimes because they do not have a clear idea of what they are supposed to be doing with their lives.

I have had many a conversation with newly retired individuals who told me that they try to find ways "to kill time" now that they no longer work full-time. I thought: These people may have twenty or thirty more years to live; should they be devising ways to "kill" this amount of time? Shouldn't they be planning something more constructive with the time that God allots them?

Life presents all of us with a question: what next? This question applies not merely to those who have retired from their job but to each individual at every stage of life. We reach one plateau, achieve a particular goal—but then what?

If we have "our eyes in our head," we are looking forward. After having achieved one level, we need to move on to another higher level. Life should not be lived passively. We should not be thinking about "killing time." Each morning when we wake up, we need to remind ourselves: And now what? What have I planned as my next step in life? What goals do I have?

Life is an ongoing process of renewal, of facing new struggles, making new discoveries. A thoughtful and pious life not only is a source of happiness to the person living such a life, but also impacts positively on others. Looking forward, keeping focus, working toward fulfillment of a mission—these qualities generate energy within us and for those with whom we have contact.

Rabbi Abraham Isaac Kook, first Ashkenazic chief rabbi of Israel, once asked: Who is on a greater spiritual level, a person on the tenth rung or the thirtieth rung of the spiritual ladder? The obvious answer would be that the person on the thirtieth rung is on a higher spiritual level. But Rabbi Kook answered: It depends which direction the person is moving. If the person on the tenth rung is climbing and growing day by day, she is spiritually alive and energized. If the person on the thirtieth rung is moving downward, she has lost spiritual elan and will continue to sink unless she can redirect upward.[1]

As we step on each rung of the ladder of life, we need to evaluate whether we are moving upward or whether we are letting ourselves move downward. With each step, we need to focus on what comes next, on how we can reach the next higher level, on how we can use the time God grants us in a meaningful and constructive way. This requires planning, self-discipline, and a focus on spiritual growth. We can succeed if "our eyes are in our head."

Fame and Immortality

Then said I in my heart: "As it happens to the fool so will it happen even to me; and why was I then more wise?" Then I said in my heart, that this also is vanity. For of the wise man even as of the fool, there is no remembrance forever; seeing that in the days to come all will long ago have been forgotten. And how must the wise man die, even as the fool. So I hated life; because the work that is wrought under the sun was grievous unto me; for all is vanity and a striving after wind.

(ECCLESIASTES 2:15–17)

During our college years, we seemed to be concerned with achieving our immortal fame. We wanted to do great things that would go down in the annals of history. One of the hypothetical questions we discussed was, if we were given the choice of dying young but having eternal fame or of living a long time but dying without having achieved great fame, which would we choose? As highly motivated college students, many chose an early death with everlasting fame (like Rabbi Yitzhak Luria or Mozart or Keats) rather than a long life that ended in a whimper.

What was—and still is for many—the lure of everlasting fame? King Solomon was troubled by fears of being forgotten, of living a life that simply faded away without leaving a trace beyond perhaps a generation or two. This fear continues to haunt societies in modern times and is especially evident in contemporary America.

A criminal justice professor at the University of Alabama, Dr. Adam Lankford, recently spoke to a group of sociologists. He attempted to understand the all-too-frequent mass shootings that take place in the United States. Although the United States represents only 5 percent of the world's population, it accounts for 31 percent of public mass shooters. Between 1966 and 2012, a total of 62 percent of school and workplace shooters were American.

While the prevalence of gun ownership in the Unites States is a contributing factor to this phenomenon, Professor Lankford suggests that aspects of American culture play a significant role:

> It's the social strains of American life—the false promise of the American dream, which guarantees a level of success that can't always be achieved through hard work and sheer willpower; the devotion to individualism and the desire for fame or notoriety.[1]

Americans grow up thinking that they can achieve great things. A 2010 survey found that 81 percent of American high school students believed they would have a "great paying job" by age twenty-five. A similar survey conducted in 2014 found that 26 percent of high schoolers expected that they would soon be famous.

But reality eventually sets in. Most people will never achieve their unrealistic expectations. They settle into a lifestyle that is below that of the "American dream." This leads to feelings of frustration and dissatisfaction with life. A small percentage of these disillusioned Americans become so alienated that they resort to acts of crime and violence. By going out in a blaze of glory, mass shooters attain the power and fame (notoriety) that they could not achieve in their lives.

Dr. Lankford's analysis is relevant not merely to mass shooters, but to all sorts of people who feel dissatisfaction with their lives. We are bombarded with images of athletes and entertainers, business moguls and con artists, who have amassed great fortunes, who live in huge mansions, who seem to have a monopoly on success. They have so much money; their names are frequently in the news; they are invited to fancy meetings with famous politicians. People ask themselves: Why do they have so much, and why do I have so little in comparison?

While the American dream prods us to achieve great things and promises us great opportunity, it also creates unrealistic goals and expectations. Very few will fulfill the exaggerated goals of the American dream, and many who do are still consumed with feelings of dissatisfaction. They wonder why they didn't achieve even more. They cast jealous eyes on those who seem to have done better. The American dream, like the end of the rainbow, seems to be eternally elusive.

We should ask: What is the ultimate value of fame? Why would people sacrifice so much to attain long-lasting glory? Once we are dead, should it really make any difference to us if people remember our names or not?

The desire for immortality is rooted in the desire to find ultimate meaning in our lives. We think that if we achieve great things, we will be remembered by future generations. That is an important validation of our lives. We want our life's energies to continue to impact future generations even if we are no longer alive. To die quietly and anonymously seems to indicate the meaninglessness of our lives. It is as though we did not live at all, as if it made no difference to humanity whether we lived or died.

Yet, as we grow older and wiser, we hopefully come to realize that the validation of our lives does not come from amorphous fame. Rather, it comes from living a meaningful and constructive life filled with love, generosity, and wisdom. If we are remembered by those whose lives we have touched, that is validation enough. We do not need the accolades of millions of people; we do not need our names to be remembered in future generations. We need to live wisely and righteously. Let fame take care of itself. We are happy with or without it.

Humor and Happiness

There is nothing better for a man than that he should eat and drink and make his soul enjoy pleasure for his labor. This also I saw that it is from the hand of God.

(ECCLESIASTES 2:24)

Behold that which I have seen: it is good, yea, it is comely for one to eat and to drink and to enjoy pleasure for all his labor wherein he labors under the sun, all the days of his life which God has given him; for this is his portion. Every man also to whom God has given riches and wealth, and has given him power to eat thereof and to take his portion and to rejoice in his labor—this is the gift of God. For let him remember the days of his life that they are not many; for God answers him in the joy of his heart.

(ECCLESIASTES 5:17–19)

Go your way, eat your bread with joy, and drink your wine with a merry heart; for God has already accepted your works. Let your garments be always white; and let your head lack no oil. Enjoy life with the wife whom you love.... For there is no work, nor device, nor knowledge, nor wisdom in the grave where you are going.

(ECCLESIASTES 9:7–10)

The Talmud (*Taanit* 22a) relates a story in which Elijah the Prophet pointed out two people who had a place in the world-to-come. Who were these outstanding individuals? They were street comedians! They told jokes. When asked why they devoted their time to making people laugh, they answered: We try to relieve people's sufferings; we offer them a moment of laughter to free them from their woes; we use humor to bring peace among those who are arguing with each other.

The eighteenth-century sage Rabbi Eliyahu ha-Cohen of Izmir elaborated on the virtues of these street comedians:

> Anyone who is happy all his days thereby indicates the greatness of his trust in God. This is why they [the street comedians] were always happy.... This quality [of accepting life with happiness] is enough to give a person merit to have a place in the world-to-come; for great is trust [in God], even if a person is not perfect in all other moral perfections." (*Midrash Talpiot*)

Religion is at its best when it contributes to our sense of happiness and well-being. Eating, drinking, and being merry are not sinful in themselves; sinfulness arises from overindulgence, from a hedonistic attitude that disregards the sacred element in our physical enjoyments.

Maimonides in his *Guide for the Perplexed* (3:43) makes a significant comment about religion and happiness:

> The festivals are all for rejoicings and pleasurable gatherings, which in most cases are indispensable for man; they are also useful in the establishment of friendship, which must exist among people living in political societies.

Happy occasions are essential. Pleasurable gatherings enlarge our lives by linking us with family and friends, by enabling us to meet new people and interact with them in a positive environment. Indeed, we not only have the festival days; we have the joy of Shabbat each week and so many mitzvoth each day. The hallmark of Jewish religious life is happiness!

In his book *Happiness and the Human Spirit*, Dr. Abraham Twerski describes what he calls "Spiritual Deficiency Syndrome." People feel a sense of malaise with their lives because they do not realize that happiness depends on a spiritual worldview. They cannot gain happiness simply by attaining more physical or material things; they will always be left wanting more. A spiritual deficiency is a lack in the development of those qualities that distinguish human beings from mere biological organisms.

Among the human characteristics that are essential for happiness is compassion, a feeling of empathy for others. Dr. Twerski, who is both a rabbi and a psychiatrist, writes:

> As a physician, I try to fix people's pain, to relieve them of their suffering. But as a rabbi, I learned to share people's pain. As advanced as modern medicine is, there are still times when I cannot fix things, but I can always share.[1]

He points out that empathic listening is a vital ingredient in living a happy and fulfilled life.

Dr. Twerski notes that those who try to control others suffer from Spiritual Deficiency Syndrome. Instead of trying to share with others, they try to control others. This reflects their basic discontent with themselves. To compensate for their poor self-image, they seek to lord over others and thereby gain status. But this strategy inevitably fails because the controller still remains discontented. Dr. Twerski notes:

> People who fulfill themselves by controlling others are caught in a vicious cycle. Because control is the antithesis of true self-fulfillment, the more we try to exert control, the less we fulfill ourselves, the greater our symptoms of Spiritual Deficiency Syndrome.[2]

King Solomon taught that our pleasures and our genuine happiness are "from the hand of God." As we develop an optimistic and spiritual worldview, we can more readily appreciate our blessings. Our sense of gratitude and well-being not only enhances our own lives, but creates greater harmony in our families and in our communities.

A Time to Be Born and
a Time to Die

To everything there is a season, a time to be born and a
time to die.

(ECCLESIASTES 3:1–2)

During the course of my forty-six years of rabbinic service, I have
spent many hours with individuals in their last months, weeks, days,
and moments of life. While all of them would have preferred to continue living in good health, most of them—unless they died relatively suddenly—came to a peaceful acceptance of death. In their
heart of hearts, they understood that they were mortal and that
death was inevitable.

I have had the amazing privilege (yes, it was a privilege) to be
with individuals in their last days of life who were actually radiant in
their serenity and calm wisdom. They were not at all afraid of death.
They knew that to everything there is a season, a time to be born
and a time to die. Their time had come. They overflowed with gratitude for the lives they had led and with love for those who were
most precious to them and who had made their lives worthwhile.

The thoughtful scientist Lewis Thomas has written that "we may
be about to rediscover that dying is not such a bad thing to do after
all." Drawing on the research done on people who seemed to have
died clinically but who then somehow came back to life, Thomas
notes:

> Those who remember parts or all of their episodes do not
> recall any fear or anguish. Several people who remained
> conscious throughout, while appearing to have been

quite dead, could only describe a remarkable sensation of detachment.[1]

Dr. Oliver Sacks, famed neurologist and author, wrote a poignant essay shortly before illness took his life. He entitled the article "Sabbath" and reminisced about his upbringing in an Orthodox, Sabbath-observing Jewish family; his subsequent alienation from Orthodoxy; and his reconciliation with his Orthodox family during the latter part of his life. He concluded his essay with a short meditation on life:

> And now, weak, short of breath, my once-firm muscles melted away by cancer, I find my thoughts, increasingly, not on the supernatural or spiritual, but on what is meant by living a good and worthwhile life—achieving a sense of peace within oneself. I find my thoughts drifting to the Sabbath, the day of rest, the seventh day of the week, and perhaps the seventh day of one's life as well, when one can feel that one's work is done, and one may, in good conscience, rest.[2]

The Talmud (*Tamid* 32a) records questions that Alexander the Great had asked a group of Rabbinic sages. Two of the questions and answers were as follows:

> Question: What should a person do in order to live?
> Answer: He should make himself die.

> Question: What should a person do in order to die?
> Answer: He should make himself live.

This enigmatic dialogue may be understood as follows: We can live an intensely meaningful life if we are aware of impending death. Recognizing our mortality leads us to value each moment, to appreciate the present, since it is so fleeting. Conversely, we should live life fully without fear of death and without becoming morose over the prospect of our mortality.

In his play *Our Town*, Thornton Wilder explores how mortals tend to pass their everyday lives without adequate appreciation of each moment. Wilder writes, "Each individual's assertion to an absolute reality can only be inner, very inner."[3] As we experience each moment with greater intensity, we validate our lives; we develop the inner wisdom to appreciate what we have and what we inevitably will lose.

To everything there is a season. The secret of a well-lived life is to value the gifts and challenges of each season.

The Haves and Have–Nots

But I returned and considered all the oppressions that
are done under the sun; and behold the tears of such as
were oppressed, and they had no comforter; and on the
side of their oppressors there was power, but they had no
comforter.

(ECCLESIASTES 4:1)

The world is, and always seems to have been, divided among the
haves and the have-nots. While many people fall somewhere in the
middle, there invariably seems to be a powerful elite group that
controls wealth and power and a huge underclass of people who
seem to lack many basic things. Some people's problem is fighting
obesity; other people's problem is finding enough food to survive.
Some people worry about their summer homes, their domestic help,
their tax loopholes; other people worry about having a roof over
their heads for the night.

While these vast inequalities may be the result of bad economic
systems and poor methods of distribution of wealth, they also may
be the result of outright oppression. Those in power manipulate
things so as to maintain their advantages. They amass fortunes on
the backs of the working poor. They exploit and cheat. The poor
cry out for help, but who listens?

The tired, the poor, the huddled masses, the homeless—they
make us uncomfortable. Compassion demands that we care for
them and help relieve their sufferings. But pragmatism pushes us
in a different direction. The beggars and the needy are nuisances,
impinging on our quality of life. They cost us money, effort, and
time. And they never seem to go away.

The needy are a weight on our consciences as individuals and as a society.

During the nineteenth century, Thomas Malthus offered a suggestion on how to deal with the burgeoning population of poor and helpless. Malthus believed that social engineers should arrange for the poor to have a high rate of mortality:

> In our towns we should make the streets narrower, crowd more people into houses, and count on the return of the plague. In the country, we should build our villages near stagnant pools, and particularly encourage settlement in all marshy and unwholesome situations.[1]

This drastic approach should strike us as being immoral and ruthless. Yet, in certain ways, our contemporary society does seem to follow the advice given by Malthus. Poor people are often concentrated in slums, out of our sight. In Malthusian terms, if the poor live in areas with a higher mortality rate, less health care, and more crime, this is part of the solution rather than part of the problem. Indeed, many people seem quite content to let the poor suffer and die, as long as they do so in their own part of town and out of our line of vision.

But if we agree that this is no solution at all, then what, after all, can be done? We spend billions of dollars on welfare and social programs, and yet the problems do not get solved. Some say: The government should deal with these problems! Social agencies and philanthropies should solve the problems! Others say: The poor and needy should help themselves. Yet others "solve" the problem by moving to an expensive area where the poor cannot afford to follow.

All of these strategies do not solve the problems, nor do they resolve the inner conflict of each moral person in our society. Expecting someone else to eliminate the crisis does not work. Running away from the problem is only a short-lived venture in escapism. The problem always follows.

For many years, our synagogue operated a shelter for homeless men. I had a conversation with one of our homeless guests, and I lamented the seeming impossibility of solving the problem of homelessness. Our homeless shelter was merely a tiny bandage; it was not curing homelessness.

The homeless person to whom I was complaining looked perplexed. He gave me some good advice: "Don't focus on the whole problem. Think of one person at a time. The shelter is keeping me warm and safe for this night. Perhaps tomorrow will be better."

None of us can solve the overall problem. None of us can relieve all the suffering, poverty, and illness in the world. But every one of us can do something. We can create a human connection with at least one person, maybe a few more. We can give contributions of money and time. We can think of the poor and downtrodden not as "them" but as part of "us."

Will this process solve all the problems? Probably not. Will we still have a moral dilemma and a troubled conscience? Very likely. And perhaps this is a true sign of a moral individual and of a moral society. Moral people face the gap between the ideal world and the real world and try to bring the two closer together. This process involves frustration, guilt, inner conflict. When we stop feeling the pain of this dilemma, we have lost a powerful moral impulse.

The Torah describes the founding national experience of the Israelites as having been slaves in Egypt. The Torah emphasizes that because we were slaves, we will be more understanding and more sympathetic to the downtrodden of the world.

For generations, the ancient Egyptians felt no moral qualms about forcing the Israelites into servitude, or murdering the Israelites' children, or seeing the daily sufferings of the Israelite slaves. When a society loses its moral conscience, it tolerates—and promotes—dehumanization of its weakest and neediest members. Moses and Aaron strove to stoke Pharaoh's moral conscience. It was a long, arduous, and painful process before the Israelites were finally allowed to go free.

A moral conscience helps us sympathize with the poor and downtrodden; it helps us maintain sensitivity to the needs of others; it prods us to do something—however small—to alleviate the pain and suffering of our fellow human beings. Each gesture of kindness is a contribution not only to the human being whom we help, but to society at large—and to our own moral development.[2]

Too often, King Solomon's complaint is true: the tears of the poor go without being comforted. Our moral challenge is to be counted among those who hear the cries of the downtrodden ... and who do something to help and to give comfort.

Essential Human Nature

Two are better than one; because they have a good reward for their labor. For if they fall, the one will lift up his fellow; but woe to him that is alone when he falls and has not another to lift him up ... and a threefold cord is not quickly broken.

(ECCLESIASTES 4: 9–10, 4:12)

Are human beings basically animals who need to be tamed by the forces of civilization? Or are we angelic beings who sometimes get dragged down by the external forces of nature?

In his writing, Thomas Hobbes drew upon the Latin proverb *Homo homini lupus*, "Man is wolf to man." We can't trust each other—or ourselves!—to act in a non-wolf-like pattern; we need to be controlled by laws, to be forced to behave morally. The role of religion and civilization is to curb our innate tendency toward aggression and violence.

On the other hand, some argue that humans are innately kind and cooperative; we descend into violent behavior because of pressures from outside ourselves, such as feeling threatened by others or living in an environment of poverty or drug addiction. If we could clean up the external negative features of society, we would all live nice, quiet, moral lives.

Proponents of the Hobbesian view draw on the notion of "survival of the fittest." According to this theory, humans (and indeed all animals) are engaged in an ongoing struggle for survival. There is a never-ending competition for resources; only the strongest prevail and reproduce. Weaker animals are killed or die out. Thus, the best strategy for survival is to destroy the competition.

Yet, this theory has been seriously challenged by a growing number of contemporary researchers. In his important writings, Frans de Waal has provided evidence to demonstrate that animals—including human beings—actually enhance their prospects for survival by cooperative behavior. By working together with others, they are better able to maintain the safety and security of their groups. In his book *The Age of Empathy*, de Waal points out that nature provides lessons for a kinder society. Being nice is not only an abstract moral principle; it is a key ingredient for survival and happiness.[1] In his book *Beyond Revenge*, Michael McCullough has described the evolution of the forgiveness instinct. Just as we have an urge to take revenge, we also have a strong streak within us that encourages us to forgive.[2]

As King Solomon observed, a cooperative relationship is a positive element in healthy living. A loyal friend can share our joys and sorrows, can stand with us in good times and bad. As our circle of friends expands, so does our ability to live a stronger and happier life. As they share with us, so we share with them; the cooperative framework enhances all of our lives.

Jewish tradition has long understood that human beings are complex, that we have both positive and negative inclinations. Judaism does not view humanity as a group of individuals struggling for survival by engaging in wolf-like aggression against others; nor does it view humanity as an innately peace-loving, altruistic group.

We like to think that we are essentially good and that we have the power to overcome our evil inclinations. The Torah instructs us to share with the poor: "You shall not harden your heart nor clench your fist from your needy brother" (Deuteronomy 15:7). Rabbi Yitzhak Shemuel Reggio, a nineteenth-century Italian Torah commentator, notes, "One who holds himself back from helping a poor and impoverished person needs to harden his heart, because compassion is part of human nature."[3] In other words, we are essentially good, compassionate individuals who naturally want to help others. Only by hardening our hearts can we overcome our natural tendency to do good.

This optimistic assessment of human nature was alluded to in a comment attributed to Rabbi Joseph B. Soloveitchik.[4] He noted that according to Freudian psychology, human beings at root are filled with animal instincts. If you scratch deeply enough into the human psyche, you will find aggressiveness, hostility, and jealousy. He contrasted this viewpoint with the classic Jewish teaching. If you go as deeply as possible into the human psyche, you will find holiness, a profound crying out for God. As the Psalmist declared, *Mimaamakim keratikha Adonai*, "From our very depths we call out to God" (Psalm 130:1).

The Torah teaches us of the obligation to do that which is upright and good, to live a morally responsible and respectable life. The optimistic Jewish view suggests that these are goals to which we are naturally disposed. We sin only if we deviate from our basic desire to live generously and compassionately. Yes, we do have negative inclinations, and yes, these inclinations can drag us down. But the hallmark of a truly religious person is the recognition that at root and in our depths we are endowed with a grand spirituality that is the key to an upright, good, and happy life.

The March of Folly

Better is a poor and wise child than an old and foolish king, who knows not how to receive admonition any
more.

(Ecclesiastes 4:13)

In her book *The March of Folly*, the historian Dr. Barbara Tuchman
describes the immorality and corruption that characterized a group
of Renaissance popes. Rodrigo Borgia, known as Pope Alexander
VI, was an egregious example of depraved and luxurious living. Late
in life, he was stricken with a moment of remorse. He told a consis-
tory of cardinals, "The most grievous danger for any Pope lies in
the fact that encompassed as he is by flatterers, he never hears the
truth about his own person and ends by not wishing to hear it."[1]

This problem is not limited to popes but applies to kings, presi-
dents, heads of corporations ... and almost anyone in a leadership
position of some kind. Those who surround themselves with fakes
and flatterers become impervious to criticism. They do not receive,
and do not want to receive, opinions that differ with their own. As
King Solomon well noted, a "poor and wise child" is better than a
"foolish king" who does not know how to receive admonition.

Dr. Tuchman tries to understand the folly of leaders, ancient and
modern. Why did they pursue policies that were self-destructive?
Why did they ignore the valid critiques of dissenters? Why did they
lead their nations and their armies into unnecessary peril? Among
the reasons, Dr. Tuchman suggests that leaders simply do not want
to admit when they have made mistakes. Their egotism prevents
them from being honest and self-reflective. In their megalomania,
they consider critics to be enemies; so the critics either remain silent
or they are maligned, isolated, or eliminated.

Folly is ubiquitous when people let their egos get in the way of good judgment. Dr. Daniel K. Kahneman, the Israeli Nobel Prize winner in economics in 2002, coined the phrase "illusion of validity."[2] His vast research into human decision making led him to the conclusion that people tend to think their decisions are valid—even when those decisions are based on first impressions or on relatively brief observations. Dr. Kahneman assembled impressive evidence demonstrating the proclivity of humans—even so-called experts—to make serious errors in judgment. People are swayed by their moods, by their personal inclinations, by the language or circumstances in which problems are presented. The best hope for attaining proper judgment is to overcome the illusion of validity, the internal feeling that we can assess things truthfully on our own. In fact, we need careful study and as much objective data as possible in order to reach sensible judgments. And as important—and perhaps more important—we need to be open to the ideas of others. Legitimate criticism is a constructive element in decision making.

People who have the illusion of validity and who shut off admonition from others are not only misguided. They are dangerous to themselves and to society.

Listening to Silence

Be not rash with your mouth, and let not your heart be hasty to utter a word before God; for God is in heaven, and you upon earth; therefore let your words be few.

(ECCLESIASTES 5:1)

Rabban Shimon ben Gamliel, a leading rabbi of Talmudic times, taught, "All my life I grew up among sages and I found that nothing is better for a person than silence" (*Pirkei Avot* 1:17). Silence is not merely the absence of words; it is a positive framework for quiet and careful thought. Our ideas and imagination develop in the silence of our minds.

One of the features of modern society is noise, a plethora of words. People seem to be afraid of silence. They want to talk and to be talked at; they want the constant buzz of a television, radio, or iPod. Talk shows are very popular with the public, even when much of the talk is banal. A person's popularity is commonly connected with garrulousness; "sociable" people love to chat.

King Solomon advised choosing one's words carefully. We should speak with the consciousness that we are speaking before God. Silly chatter, gossip, vulgarity are out of place in a conversation in the presence of the Almighty—so they should always be out of place! A wise person thinks before speaking and chooses words carefully.

Not only should we foster the virtue of silence in ourselves, we should appreciate the silence in the minds and hearts of others. Just as we pay heed to the words uttered by others, so we should be sensitive to their unstated feelings.

The Torah informs us that the people of Israel sang a beautiful song praising God for having redeemed them from the Egyptian warriors who pursued them to the Red Sea. The song of Moses and the Israelites is written in an unusual fashion in the Torah scroll. Its words do not run together as an uninterrupted block of text but are arranged with a blank space following each clause. This style of gaps interspersed with the words implies that silence was an integral part of the song. We are to pay attention not only to the words, but to the unspoken thoughts and feelings of the Israelites. Yes, they were singing words of praise to God for their miraculous salvation. But in the silence of their souls, they also must have had fears and anxieties. How will we survive in the wilderness? How will we care for our children and for our elders? Will we be facing enemies on the road to the Promised Land? How will we adjust ourselves to a radically new reality of being free people rather than slaves?

The "Song of Moses" is important both for its words and for its gaps of silence.

So it is with life in general. We know that the words we speak represent one level of our being; the silence that often undergirds those words represents another—deeper—level. It is possible to speak words of happiness and encouragement while feeling sadness and heartbreak. It is possible to express sorrow and grief while feeling consolation and calmness within. Silent stirrings within us—and within others—must be acknowledged. To be spiritually and morally whole, we need to be closely attuned to hidden motives and meanings.

Human communication is hampered not only when words are misunderstood but when silent feelings and underlying motives go undetected. One cannot really understand a fellow human being without being prepared to invest the time and sensitivity to listen to the entire communication, verbal and nonverbal.

Cultivating silence in ourselves is a key to wisdom and creativity. Listening for the silence in others is a key to empathy and love.

Rich but Unsatisfied

He who loves silver shall not be satisfied with silver; nor he who loves abundance, with increase; this also is vanity.

(ECCLESIASTES 5:9)

Sweet is the sleep of a laboring man, whether he eat little or much; but the satiety of the rich will not suffer him to sleep.

(ECCLESIASTES 5:11)

The psychologist David Myers in his book *The American Paradox: Spiritual Hunger in an Age of Plenty* points out that the physical conditions of Americans have improved dramatically over the years; yet, Americans don't seem to have become happier. Since 1960, the U.S. divorce rate has doubled, the teen suicide rate has tripled, the recorded violent crime rate has quadrupled, the prison population has quintupled. The rate of serious clinical depression has more than tripled over the last two generations and increased by perhaps a factor of ten from 1900 to 2000.[1]

People live under the mistaken notion that if only they had more money, they would be happier. They do not realize that happiness comes from within the self, not from the accumulation of dollars. Having material assets does not necessarily mean having emotional strength.

We have all known rich people who are insecure, or who have serious personal and family problems, or who are bent on living ostentatiously in order to show off their wealth. We know—and they probably also know—that they are not living healthy, happy lives. They are in a self-imposed rat race that gives them the illusion of success and power.

We have also known hardworking poor and middle-class people who refuse to enter the rat race but who live happily and without pretensions. They understand the profound truth that genuine happiness is determined not by one's financial assets but by one's spiritual assets.

It takes courage to step out of the rat race and to see life on a grander scale. It is tempting to accept the materialistic values of society and to try to win by playing the game by the rules of the rat race. Some people insist on buying only designer clothes, preferably from the most fashionable and expensive stores. If they do not wear exactly the "right" clothes that will make the "right" impression on others, they feel ugly and ashamed. On their deathbeds, will such people still think that devotion to designer clothing was essential to living the good life?

Society is filled with those who are jealous, greedy, power hungry, rude, arrogant. They crave recognition; they want to demonstrate their superiority to the hoi polloi; they feel pain if others have more than they do. They want to be part of the "right" clique.

People in the rat race are not necessarily foolish or evil. They simply have not allowed themselves to think carefully about the meaning of life. They have allowed others to set the agenda for their lives. But they may wake up one morning and ask: Why am I letting my life fritter away as I chase after illusory goals? How can I get back to my basic self?

Pirkei Avot offers good advice:

> Do not seek greatness for yourself and do not long for honor. Let your deeds exceed your learning. Do not crave the table of kings, for your table is greater than theirs, your crown is greater than their crown, and your Employer can be relied upon to pay you your labor's reward. (*Pirkei Avot* 6:5)

Greatness and honors are by-products of a life of good deeds and personal fulfillment. They are not ends in themselves; to pursue them is the sign of a flawed philosophy of life. If we live a good, upright life, we do not need to sit at the table of kings in order to have our life validated. When we are satisfied to serve God humbly and honestly, we do not need public accolades.

Willy Loman and Us

All the labor of man is for his mouth, and yet the appetite
is not filled.

(ECCLESIASTES 6:7)

Some years ago, my wife and I attended a Broadway revival of
Arthur Miller's *Death of a Salesman*, with Brian Dennehy playing
Willy Loman. By the end of the production, many of us in the audience found ourselves sobbing and with tears in our eyes. Few if any
members of the audience were traveling salesmen; few if any lived
such a frustrating, tragic life as did Willy Loman. Yet, the dramatic
power of this play touched us in a deep way.

Why?

Willy is a traveling salesman with big dreams. He seeks to be well
liked, financially secure, loved by his wife and children. But as he
grows older, his dreams crumble. He is making fewer and fewer
sales; the grueling travels are wearing him down. New buyers are
coming into their own, and they do not know Willy as had the earlier generation of buyers. He is not as well liked as he once was (or
thought he was). He is reduced to borrowing money to pay basic
expenses. His two sons grow up, and he is not at all confident of
their love. On the contrary, a palpable tension sours their relationship. Willy's wife, Linda, is as loyal and loving as any woman could
be; yet she cannot provide Willy with the fulfillment of his big
dreams. She tries her best, but Willy is beyond help. He poses as a
successful and well-liked salesman, but he knows that in reality he
is an abysmal failure. By the end of the play, Willy concludes that
he is worth more to his family if he were to die; they can then col-
lect his life insurance. "Funny, y'know? After all the highways and
the trains and the appointments and the years, you end up worth

more dead than alive." He drives off, gets into an "accident," and dies. Outside his immediate family and his neighbor, no one shows up for the funeral.

In act 1, Linda tries to get her sons to understand their father's dilemma so that they might give him the moral support he needs so desperately. "I don't say he's a great man. Willy Loman never made a lot of money. His name was never in the paper. He's not the finest character that ever lived. But he's a human being, and a terrible thing is happening to him. So attention must be paid. He's not to be allowed to fall into his grave like an old dog. Attention, attention must be finally paid to such a person."

But the sons do not pay due attention to their father's plight, and neither does anyone else except Linda. So Willy continues to sink and finally is driven to suicide. The play ends with a "requiem." Linda is perplexed and angered. Why did Willy have to end it like that? "I can't understand it. At this time especially. First time in thirty-five years we were just about free and clear. He only needed a little salary. He was even finished with the dentist." Their neighbor Charley replies, "No man only needs a little salary." Biff, Willy and Linda's son, comments, "He had the wrong dreams. All, all wrong.... He never knew who he was." And Charley then speaks with emotion: "Nobody dast blame this man. You don't understand: Willy was a salesman.... He's a man way out there in the blue, riding on a smile and a shoeshine. And when they start not smiling back—that's an earthquake.... A salesman is got to dream, boy. It comes with the territory."

The play ends with Linda speaking to Willy's grave. She can't cry. She can't understand why he killed himself. "I made the last payment on the house today. Today, dear. And there'll be nobody home. We're free and clear. We're free ... We're free ... We're free."

Vanity of vanities, all is vanity! A life of hard work and big dreams comes to nothing, Instead of the joy of freedom in life, there is the sadness of freedom in death.

Perhaps we cry at Willy Loman's tragic life out of sympathy for him and his family. But perhaps we cry because we see something of Willy Loman in ourselves.

Surely, we are more successful, happier, and more well liked than Willy was. But perhaps we hear Biff's words about Willy, and we take them to heart, at least a bit. "He had the wrong dreams.... He never knew who he was."

We work and toil to get ahead in life, without wondering if we are in fact pursuing the wrong dreams, without really knowing who we are. We devote precious time and energy to things that will make us appear important and successful, but when we look back on our lives, will we say that we chose correctly? Did we have the right dreams? Did we know who we were? Did we labor relentlessly without ever really feeling satisfied?

The story of Willy Loman puts a mirror up to our own lives. It poignantly underscores how a human being can fail at life by making the wrong choices, by having the wrong goals, by not knowing who he is, by not understanding who she is.

"So attention must be paid. He's not to be allowed to fall into his grave like an old dog. Attention, attention must be finally paid to such a person."

Becoming Human

A good name is better than precious oil; and the day of death than the day of one's birth. It is better to go to the house of mourning than to go to the house of feasting; for that is the end of all men, and the living will lay it to his heart. Vexation is better than laughter; for by the sadness of the countenance the heart may be gladdened. The heart of the wise is in the house of mourning, but the heart of fools is in the house of mirth.

(ECCLESIASTES 7:1–4)

In what sense can the day of death be considered better than the day of one's birth? The Midrash (*Ecclesiastes Rabbah* 7:4) offers an interesting perspective. Normally, when a baby is born, everyone rejoices; when a person dies, people mourn. But shouldn't our reactions be different? When a baby is born, we have no idea how its life will unfold. Will she grow up to be happy, healthy, and righteous? Will his life be one of comfort or suffering? Since we do not know the future of a baby, birth should be a time for anxiety rather than joy. On the other hand, when a person dies, we now have the full story of that life. If the person had lived a fine, upstanding life, we should rejoice that her life was happy and successful, that his life was marked by blessing and goodness.

The Midrash offers a parable. When a ship leaves port, we are filled with trepidation. Will it reach its destination? Will the seas be calm or rough? Will the ship be strong enough to weather the storms that may befall it? But when the ship arrives at its destination, we rejoice that it has fulfilled its mission successfully. So it should be with a human's life and death. When a person "sets sail" at birth, we should be anxious; but when he arrives at his

48

destination—that is, death—we should be grateful that he achieved his mission.

"A good name is better than precious oil": Only after the life story has been completed is it possible to determine if the person has left behind a good name. Precious oil is diminished with time; a good name grows more precious with the passage of time as our memory impacts positively on those our lives have touched.

This insight is more readily gained in a house of mourning than in a place of mirth. During the mourning period, family and friends come together. They reminisce, they ponder the ups and downs of the deceased's life. If they are wise, they extrapolate from this single instance of death to the more general rhythms of life and death. They meditate on the transience of life. They realize that much of life is frittered away in foolishness and silly laughter that ultimately mean nothing. Upon contemplating death, they are enabled to clarify their own goals and ideals: How can they best use the time allotted to them to establish a good name that will endure as a blessing and inspiration to those who come afterward?

The wise King Solomon taught that awareness of our mortality is a key ingredient to a wise and meaningful life. Indeed, the importance of this awareness is highlighted in the first chapters of the Torah. Let us look more closely at the story of the first human beings recorded in the Bible.

God placed Adam and Eve in the Garden of Eden and gave them the following instruction: "Of every tree of the garden you may freely eat; but of the tree of the knowledge of good and evil you shall not eat of it; for in the day that you eat of it you shall surely die" (Genesis 2:16–17). It did not take long, though, for Adam and Eve to eat of this forbidden fruit, having been tempted by the serpent to do so. But they did not die upon eating the fruit of the tree of knowledge of good and evil.

Instead of punishing them with immediate death, God informed them of serious changes about to befall them. To Eve, God said, "I will greatly multiply your pain and travail; in pain will you bring forth children" (Genesis 3:16). To Adam, God said, "By the sweat of your brow shall you eat bread until you return unto the ground;

for out of it you were taken; for dust you are and unto dust shall you return" (Genesis 3:19).

What do these things have to do with the transgression? Since the sin was eating a forbidden fruit, Adam and Eve's punishment might more appropriately have been to suffer pains when eating or to be afflicted with digestive disorders. Why should Eve now have to deal with pain during childbirth? Why should Adam now have to toil as he farmed for his own food? Why is he told that he is dust and will return to dust? How do these "punishments" fit the "crime"?

Perhaps this story needs to be understood not in terms of sin and punishment, but as a fundamental transition in the nature of humanity. Before eating of the tree of knowledge of good and evil, Adam and Eve existed in a quasi-conscious state. They were clearly on a higher spiritual/intellectual level than animals, but their basic needs were provided for them without their having to work or to plan ahead. Just as animals graze along from day to day without self-consciousness, so Adam and Eve were not self-conscious of their nakedness or of their mortality. Upon eating from the tree of knowledge of good and evil, they suddenly became aware of death. They did not physically die at that moment, but they became starkly conscious of death.

God then informed them of the consequences of their new knowledge. When animals give birth, they may experience physical pain, but this pain is simply a natural and temporary discomfort. The animal gives birth and then recovers without an afterthought. But God informs Eve that she is not like the other animals; she has now become a conscious human being. She now must understand that when she suffers the pains of childbirth, her own life will be endangered.

When animals want to eat, they graze on what is readily available. Now God informs Adam that he is not like the other animals; he has become a conscious human being. If he wants to eat and to provide for his wife and family, he will have to work the fields; he will have to sweat, to plan, to worry. If he does not cultivate his food supply properly, he and his family will face starvation and death.

According to this interpretation, Adam and Eve before eating the forbidden fruit were in a state of prehuman consciousness. Only after eating from the fruit did they emerge as human beings aware of their mortality, aware of their responsibilities, aware of dangers that confronted them. They now realized clearly that they are dust and will return to dust.

If eating of the fruit of the tree of knowledge was an essential step in the transition into developing a human consciousness, why then had God forbidden it? Perhaps the Almighty wanted Adam and Eve to first spend a period of time in the Garden of Eden and then gradually develop their human consciousness in a slower, more organic way. If they were to eat of the tree of knowledge of good and evil at a later time, they may have been better prepared to handle the challenges of being mortal human beings.

Significantly, after Adam and Eve were informed of the consequences of their having eaten the forbidden fruit, the very next verse in the Torah informs us, "And the man called his wife's name Eve, because she was the mother of all living" (Genesis 3:20). If Adam and Eve had just been informed of terrible punishments, this would be a very strange reaction from Adam. We might have expected him to ask for God's mercy, to request that God reverse the punishment.

Yet, if we understand this episode as the dawning of human consciousness in the minds of Adam and Eve, we appreciate that they did not want to revert to their former state of preconsciousness. They were beginning to internalize the message that they were now thinking human beings with great responsibilities on their shoulders. This was a daunting message ... but also an empowering one. Adam now referred to his wife as "the mother of all living" because she was to be the matriarch of a new progeny of human beings who would live with all the strengths and weaknesses of being aware of their own mortality.

The Torah informs us that God placed cherubim to guard the tree of life, with a flaming sword circling the tree in every direction. He did not want Adam and Eve to eat from this tree, although it had not previously been forbidden to them. As long as Adam and

Eve were unaware of their mortality, eating from the tree of life would make no difference. But now that they were fully conscious of the reality of death, it would be retrogressive to allow them to eat from the tree of life and to return to a life that seemed to be eternal.

Living with the knowledge of one's mortality makes life more intense, more precious. Each moment is a gift; once it passes, it cannot be retrieved. Living as thoughtful mortals entails an appreciation of the transience of life, the importance of valuing our lives and the lives of others and our ultimate dependence on God.

Yes, this knowledge can be frightening, but it is at the root of what makes us truly human.

Life Isn't Always Fair

All things have I seen in the days of my vanity; there is a righteous man who perishes in his righteousness, and there is a wicked man who prolongs his life in his evil-doing.

(ECCLESIASTES 7:15)

There is a vanity which is done upon the earth, that there are righteous men unto whom it happens according to the work of the wicked; again, there are wicked men to whom it happens according to the work of the righteous.... So I commended mirth that a man has no better thing under the sun than to eat and to drink and to be merry, and that this should accompany him in his labor all the days of his life which God has given him under the sun.

(ECCLESIASTES 8:14–15)

I returned and saw under the sun that the race is not to the swift, nor the battle to the strong, neither yet bread to the wise, nor yet riches to men of understanding, nor yet favor to men of skill; but time and chance happen to them all.

(ECCLESIASTES 9:11)

Life is not always fair. Good people suffer. Bad people prosper. This is an age-old dilemma that has puzzled religious people for millennia. Our forefather Abraham verbalized the human expectation of a just God: "Will the Judge of all the earth not do justice?" (Genesis 18:25). When injustice prevails, it calls into question God's control of human affairs.

Yet, the issue might better be considered from another angle. God's infinite wisdom provided human beings with free will. Most of the good and the evil we experience emanate from human action or inaction. God does not make wars, human beings do! God does not cheat in business, human beings do! God does not oppress the weak, human beings do! If much of the world's population is hungry, it is not because God has imposed hunger on them; it is because human beings have not effectively distributed food to them. If vicious people amass fortunes while honest people go poor, God has not ordained this; rather, human beings have chosen not to create proper frameworks for moral and righteous societies.

When we see injustices and face moral obstacles, it is wise not to blame God, but to look to ourselves. A book by Inda Schaenen offers poignant comments by fourth graders from a wide variety of schools in Missouri. One of the students, who attends a Catholic school, offered an interesting observation: "I'd say God shows you the obstacles that you need to pass but He doesn't tell you how to pass them. He has you pass 'em by yourself. He teaches you how to learn."[1]

This fourth-grade girl has verbalized an important theological insight. God does not tell us directly how to confront challenges and obstacles. God has us deal with these things on our own. But God does endow us with the intelligence and judgment that will help guide us through our dilemmas in the best possible way.

One response to the dilemmas of life is to concentrate on our own pleasures and avoid getting involved in the problems of humanity. Seek entertainment; ignore the cries of the widows and orphans, the hungry and the oppressed—that is the haunting response of vacuous people who are part of humanity's problem, not part of the solution to our many problems.

The great philosophical question is not whether we can have faith in God. The great question is, can we have faith in humankind, in ourselves?

Tablets: Shattered and Whole

For there is not a righteous man upon earth that does
good, and sins not.

(ECCLESIASTES 7:20)

No one is perfect; but some people try harder than others to overcome their sins.

No one goes through life without suffering at least some failures
and setbacks; but some people are crushed by defeat, while others
bounce back.

The Torah prescribes one day a year, Yom Kippur, as a time for
repentance. Jewish law and ethical literature remind us that every
day is suitable for repentance, but Yom Kippur is a specially sanctified day to ensure that we engage in serious repentance at least once
a year.

Even as we repent on Yom Kippur, we know in advance that we
will have to repent again next Yom Kippur. It is inevitable that we
will sin whether intentionally or unintentionally. The price of having
free will is the certainty of making wrong choices.

The glory of the laws of repentance is in their candid recognition
that life is a spiritual struggle. Rather than to deny human fallibility,
these laws encourage us to accept our periodic transgressions and
errors in judgment ... and then move on.

Rabbinic tradition offers important guidance on how to cope
with our sins. It points to the two sets of tablets of the Law that
the Israelites received at Mount Sinai. The first set was given with
much fanfare. Yet, when Moses found the Israelites worshiping the
golden calf, he threw down the stone tablets and shattered them
into pieces. He then ascended the mountain a second time, after
which he brought down the second set of tablets of the Law.

The Talmud (*Berakhot* 8b) reports the tradition that both sets of tablets—the shattered and the whole—were kept in the ark in the Tabernacle, the sanctuary that accompanied the Israelites during their trek in the wilderness. The Talmud infers that we should show honor to elderly sages who have forgotten their Torah due to their mental decline in old age. Just as we honored them when they were "whole," so we are to honor them when they are "shattered." The shattered tablets and the whole tablets are revered.

Perhaps we can draw another lesson from the placement of both sets of tablets in the ark. Each individual has strengths, virtues, accomplishments. These reflect us at our best, when we are "whole." But each individual also has weaknesses, moral blemishes, failures. These reflect the "shatterings" within us. What are we to do with our failures?

One approach is to ignore our shortcomings and concentrate only on our strengths. This is the way of egocentrism and arrogance. Another approach is to focus on our shortcomings to such an extent that we become guilt-ridden and self-hating. This is the way of negativity, making us feel powerless and unworthy.

We are called upon to store both sets of tablets within our holy arks—our inner selves. We recognize our good qualities, but we do not disdain our failures. We bring our "shattered" selves along with our "intact" selves. We learn from our errors. If we are contrite about foolish decisions and missed opportunities, we cannot let these failings crush us, but neither can we go on with our lives as though they never happened. We live as "whole" human beings when we can integrate our virtues and vices, our strengths and weaknesses, our successes and failures. The "whole" tablets remind us of how good we can be. The "shattered" tablets remind us how we have sometimes fallen short—but how we can regain our footing and do better next time.

The ark in the Tabernacle held both sets of tablets of the Law, just as our inner selves hold both sets of our own personal tablets of our lives. Ultimately, this strategy teaches us humility as well as confidence; it teaches us to look to our strengths but not to forget our weaknesses; it helps us strive to become whole human beings.[1]

Being Natural, Not Pretentious

Be not righteous overmuch; neither make yourself overwise; why should you destroy yourself?

(ECCLESIASTES 7:16)

Behold this only have I found, that God made man
upright; but they have sought out many inventions.

(ECCLESIASTES 7:29)

When I was a boy, I and so many others of my generation were avid
fans of Mickey Mantle and Willie Mays. We admired them not just
because they were great batters, base runners, and outfielders. We
admired them because they were so amazingly natural and graceful.

They seemed to have an instinct; as soon as a batter connected
with a baseball, they were already running into position to catch
the fly ball. They made catches look easy where other players would
have had to make leaping catches or would have missed altogether.
They made difficult plays look relatively routine.

All really great players are spontaneous and natural. Lesser players seem to try too hard. This is true not only of baseball but of
all areas of human endeavor. The really great and exceptional people are the ones who do amazing things in a natural, inconspicuous way. Those who are constantly striving to show how good they
are—those are the ones who invariably are not of the first rank.
They play to the grandstands, they seek popular adulation; but they
lack the inner poise and serenity that come with real greatness.

This is true also when it comes to religion. Alan Watts, who
wrote many books on Eastern religion, made an important observation relevant to all religions:

> The most spiritual people are the most human. They are natural and easy in manner; they give themselves no airs; they interest themselves in ordinary everyday matters, and are not forever talking and thinking about religion. For them there is no difference between spirituality and usual life.[1]

The highest expression of religiosity is manifested in natural, graceful, inconspicuous piety. Jewish folk tradition speaks of thirty-six hidden righteous people upon whom the existence of the world depends. These individuals are hidden; no one—not even they themselves—recognizes them as being in the elite group of *tzaddikim*. Their piety is so total and so natural that no one notices it!

Jewish law frowns on *yuhara*—pretentious religious behavior. It sees such behavior as expressions not of true religiosity, but of egotism or misguided piety. Rabbi Eliezer Papo (1785–1828; Silistra, Bulgaria) in his book of Jewish ethics *Pele Yoetz* wrote:

> If you wish to adopt a practice that the law does not require, observe it privately. This is especially true of a person who is not stringent in all his activities.... God knows a person's heart. If one acts piously in secret, God will judge him favorably. Even a person known to be pious should not perform acts of excessive piety which the leaders of the generation do not do. People will say, "This person, who acts more strictly than our sages and saints, is pretentious!"[2]

Religious observance sometimes gives the impression of trying too hard, of seeking to make a public impression. There is an emphasis on external dress and a stress on adopting extra stringencies. Instead of being natural, graceful, and unpretentious in their religiosity, some adopt behavior patterns that strive to catch people's attention. They want to be known as being extremely pious, but by doing so, they slip into the vice of pretentiousness.[3]

King Solomon warned against being "overwise" and seeking out "many inventions." Religiosity and goodness are best when they are quiet, humble, and unpretentious. Life is not about impressing others, but about being faithful and true in the eyes of God.

As You Judge, So You Will Be Judged

He who digs a pit shall fall into it; and whoso breaks through a fence, a serpent shall bite him.

(ECCLESIASTES 10:8)

A sad but recurring fact of life is that people do not always act nicely and compassionately. We come across unscrupulous, cruel, and vindictive individuals who have the power to hurt and oppress, to squeeze out illegal profits, to crush those who stand in their way.

But these people are failures at life, even if they think they are winners. They ultimately lose the respect and trust of others, even of their closest relatives and friends. If they have any degree of realism, they also come to lose respect for themselves. And in the long run, they will one day face the Judge of all judges, the One True Judge who cannot be fooled or bribed. They devise ways to hurt others or to rob them, but these plans backfire on them. They themselves become victims of their own unseemly behavior.

King Solomon's admonition echoes that of his father King David: "He digs a pit and digs it deep, but he himself will fall into the hole he has made. His mischief will recoil upon his own head, his violence will come down upon his own skull" (Psalm 7:16–17).

It is particularly sad when individuals who claim to be religious act in a vindictive and mean way. For example, when a Jewish marriage has fallen apart and the husband refuses to grant his wife a religious divorce (*get*), this is a classic example of antireligious behavior. Such a man is driven by revenge, a sense of personal failure, a desire to hurt his wife. A man who creates this situation may feel that he is demonstrating his power. In fact, though, such a man is morally deficient. Who could ever trust such a man in the future?

Who would want to associate with such a defective human being? Who would want to trust such a man in any context? The man who immorally withholds a *get* forfeits his good name in this world and will have to answer to the Almighty in the next world.

When a marriage has ended in divorce and one party or the other attempts to alienate the children from their mother or father, this is a serious and unhealthy situation. For the sake of the welfare of the children, divorced spouses need to find ways to create an amicable arrangement. One does not "win" by alienating children from their mother or father. One does not "win" by finding ways to punish a divorced spouse. Unless there are circumstances where the divorced spouse is a danger to the children's lives, each spouse needs to be compassionate and respectful. Vindictiveness does the children a disservice.

The Mishnah (*Sotah* 1:7) teaches that we will be subject to the same standard of judgment that we use in judging others. The Almighty will exact retribution in consonance with our own standards of judgment. If we willfully harm another, the heavenly court will exact payment. If we see injustice but look aside, the heavenly court will look aside when passing judgment on our soul. If we have betrayed the trust of others, we can expect exact retribution when facing divine justice. There are no free rides: cruelty, injustice, vindictiveness, and betrayal will all be repaid, measure for measure.

On the other hand, if we are righteous and compassionate, we will be repaid accordingly. The great Hasidic master Rabbi Levi Yitzhak of Berdichev was famous for finding virtue and merit in everyone, even those who were unworthy of such kindness. He is said to have prayed to the Almighty, "O merciful Father, please have mercy on me as I have had mercy on my fellow human beings; please show me compassion as I have shown compassion to all."

The Jerusalem Talmud (end of the tractate *Peah*) relates that a blind man came to town and the prominent sage Rabbi Eliezer sat next to him. When the community saw that Rabbi Eliezer showed such honor to the blind man, people assumed that the visitor must be a person of importance. They provided generous sustenance to him. The blind man inquired why he had merited such wonderful care. He was told that Rabbi Eliezer had sat next to him and this caused the public to hold the visitor in high esteem. The blind man then offered a blessing to Rabbi Eliezer: "You have shown compassion to one who is seen but who does not see. May the One who sees and is not seen receive your prayers and shower compassion on you."

We are each challenged to recognize that we will be judged and treated by the same standards with which we conduct our lives. May we be worthy to offer this prayer: "May the One who sees and is not seen receive our prayers and shower compassion on us."

Goodness and Ingratitude

Cast your bread upon the waters, for you shall find it
after many days.

(ECCLESIASTES 11:1)

King Solomon teaches that if you invest in an act of kindness, you will
be duly rewarded after many days. Your goodness will not be in vain.

Surely, we can point to examples of times when we have helped
those in need and then later—even many years later—these ben-
eficiaries of our kindness have shown their gratitude to us. The
Midrash (*Ecclesiastes Rabbah* 11:1) reports that a Roman was
washed ashore after a shipwreck. Bar Kappara, a leading sage of
the time, took the Roman home, clothed him, fed him, and cared
for him until he was able to go on his way. Years later, the Roman
government imposed heavy penalties on the Jews, and Bar Kappara went to Rome in order to plead on behalf of his community.
It turned out that the Roman governor was none other than the
man Bar Kappara had assisted after the shipwreck. The Roman recognized the rabbi and, in appreciation of his past kindness, relieved
the Jews of the harsh decrees.

Yet, although such stories certainly support King Solomon's optimistic viewpoint, we also can point to examples of times when we
have helped others and received no reward at all. On the contrary, in
return for our goodness, we have been repaid with ingratitude and
abuse. A popular quip has it that no good deed goes unpunished—
and there is a lot of truth in this witticism.

A Judeo-Spanish proverb advises: *Aze bueno y echalo a la mar*,
"Do a good deed, and cast it into the ocean." The idea is, do what
is right and don't expect any thanks or reward. The motivation for
doing good is the doing good itself, not the anticipation of gratitude or benefit. Nevertheless, deep down in our hearts, it is difficult
not to feel hurt if our goodness is not acknowledged.

In *Notes from the Underground*, Fyodor Dostoevsky's narrator says:

> I'm even inclined to believe that the best definition of man is—a creature who walks on two legs and is ungrateful. But that is not all, that is not his principal failing; his greatest failing is his constant lack of moral sense ... and, consequently, lack of good sense.

Ingratitude is related to a lack of moral sense, a lack of good sense. A person who receives a benefit should naturally and spontaneously express appreciation to the benefactor. It is not merely good manners, it is simple decency. Although the benefactor should not expect thanks, the recipient should naturally feel motivated to give thanks.

Yet, we all sense the truth of Dostoevsky's definition of man as a creature who is ungrateful. Ingratitude may simply be the result of carelessness or thoughtlessness or from a sense of being entitled to things without having to say thanks.

Humanity seems to be plagued with what I call the "paper towel syndrome," where people are used and then unceremoniously cast aside. As long as a person is deemed productive or useful, he is respected. But once the person has been fully exploited, she is put aside and forgotten, cast into the trash bin of human history. No one says thanks any longer; no one even gives her a second thought. *Aze bueno y echalo a la mar*, "Do a good deed, and cast it into the ocean." There is no point expecting gratitude or appreciation. Ingratitude is a hard fact of life. Do good ... and that is its own reward.

At the root of ingratitude is a basic arrogance, a self-absorbed view of life—an essential lack of humility. Egotists use others to advance their own goals, and they are quick to discard people once they are no longer of use to them. Egotists validate Dostoevsky's observation that human beings are characterized by ingratitude, lack of moral sense, lack of common sense.[1]

"Cast your bread upon the waters, for you shall find it after many days." But even if you never do find it, cast your bread upon the waters without expectation of reward. Do what is good and right because it is good and right. That is its own reward.

When There Is Life—Live!

In the morning sow your seed, and in the evening withhold not your hand; for you know not which shall prosper, whether this or that, or whether they both shall be alike good.

(ECCLESIASTES 11:6)

Sometimes, people give up on their lives. They reach retirement age and may have twenty or thirty years of life ahead of them, but for all practical purposes, they are simply treading water until death greets them. They sit in front of their televisions or play golf or bask in the sunshine.

King Solomon wisely taught that we must live each stage of our lives in a constructive way. As long as we have goals and aspirations, we are alive; we are growing; we are utilizing the gift of time in a meaningful way. The Talmud reports that Rabbi Akiva had thousands of students, many of whom perished in a plague or war. In response to this overwhelming tragedy, Rabbi Akiva attracted thousands more students and started again to impart his Torah wisdom to a new generation. He did not give up on life. Whether in the morning or evening of our lives, there is work to be done, things to be accomplished. We may indeed have greater success in the work we do later in life than we had in our younger days.

It is instructive to remember that Moses was eighty years old when God called upon him to go and liberate the Israelites from Egypt. For the previous many years, Moses had been a simple shepherd; now, as a man two-thirds of the way through his life, he emerged as an incredible leader who left a lasting imprint on all subsequent human history.

When Moses demanded that Pharaoh release the Israelites so that they could worship God, he insisted, "We will go with our young and with our old, with our sons and with our daughters" (Exodus 10:9). A Hasidic interpretation of Moses's words plays on the Hebrew: *binareinu uvizkeineinu nelekh* (we will go with our young and with our old). Instead of translating *binareinu* as "with our young," it is translated as "with our youth." The meaning is that even as we advance in years, we carry our own youth within us— that is, we retain the enthusiasm and idealism of our younger days. We may appear to be old physically, but mentally and emotionally we are still energized by our own inner child.

In his book *Late Bloomers*, Brendan Gill cites numerous examples of people who launched new and productive careers in their older years.[1] Oscar Hammerstein was sixty-four when he wrote the lyrics to *The Sound of Music*. Michelangelo was seventy-two when he designed the dome of Saint Peter's Basilica in Rome. Frank Lloyd Wright was ninety-one when he completed work on the Guggenheim Museum. A great many lesser-known individuals have made remarkable achievements while elderly. What is their secret? They carry their youthfulness within! They are filled with wonder, with creativity; they want to keep learning and keep growing and keep testing their ideas.

Rabbi Dr. Abraham Twerski in his book *Happiness and the Human Spirit* advises readers "The key is to think of self-fulfillment in terms of effort rather than outcome. All we can do is make the best effort possible."[2] It is all too easy to avoid undertaking new challenges due to fear of anticipated failure. People think: I'm too old, I will never finish this task, I don't have it within me to succeed any further. But this type of thinking is self-destructive. It saps life of meaning and happiness. Rather, one should rally the inner child to take a chance, to try to undertake something grand and challenging. Dr. Twerski wisely reminds us that our responsibility is to exert our best effort and not to be overly daunted by the possible outcome.

The Hasidic interpretation focuses on *binareinu*, but we should also pay attention to *uvizkeineinu*. Although normally translated as "with our old," we might also understand this as a charge to each person, regardless of age, to imagine his older years yet to come. How would I deal with this problem if I were much older than I am now? What wisdom or experience could I bring to this new situation? If I were to look at my present life as though I were nearing life's end, how would I judge myself? What would I do differently?

It has often been said that no one on his deathbed looks back on life and says, "I wish I had spent more time in my office!" If we imagine ourselves to be looking back on our lives, we can often gain important perspective on how to live our present lives more meaningfully.

When we seek freedom and the fulfillment of our spiritual natures, we need to draw on our inner youthfulness and on our anticipated elderly mature vision. Seeing our own lives through the prism of our past and our future helps us to live righteously and happily.

"We will go with our young and with our old," said Moses to Pharaoh. Good advice, even today!

Koheleth's Ultimate Insights

The end of the matter, all having been heard: fear God and keep His commandments, for this is the whole of man. For God will bring every work into the judgment concerning every hidden thing, whether it be good or whether it be evil.

(ECCLESIASTES 12:13–14)

The wise King Solomon devoted tremendous effort trying to understand the meaning of life. He was blessed with health, wealth, wisdom, power ... and yet he still felt a void within himself. When pondering the eternal rhythms of nature, the mortality of all living beings, and the essential insignificance of human life, he wondered if life was simply vanity and striving after wind or if it had some lasting purpose.

In her book *Passages*, Gail Sheehy offers reflections reminiscent of the musings of Ecclesiastes. Describing her internal voice as she was thirty-five years old, she writes, "Some intruder shook me by the psyche and shouted: *Take stock! Half your life has been spent.... You have been a performer, not a full participant. And now you are thirty-five.*"[1] She confronts herself with a startling observation: "*You've done some good work, but what does it really add up to?*"[2] Sheehy's book relates to the natural wonderings and doubts that we have at the various stages of our lives. If we understand the inner challenges that face us as we proceed through the passages of life, we can cope with them more intelligently.

Ecclesiastes has raised the questions and self-doubts that people have had from time immemorial. All thoughtful people have asked at various stages of their lives: does it really add up to anything?

By the end of Ecclesiastes, King Solomon seems to have come to a resolution: don't worry about the grand cosmic view of things; just concentrate on everyday life. There is no point in putting our lives into the context of eternity; rather, we must focus on each moment.

In his discussion of Ecclesiastes, Rabbi Harold Kushner mulls over Solomon's ultimate resolution of the conundrum of life:

> My mind tells me to give up my quest for meaning because there isn't any. All of my experience points in the same direction. But something from deeper inside me wells up and overrules my mind, dismissing the evidence and insists that in spite of all, a human life has to mean something. And that feeling, says Ecclesiastes, is why I am a human being and not an animal.... If logic tells us that life is a meaningless accident, says Ecclesiastes at the end of his journey, don't give up on life. Give up on logic.[3]

"Fear God": Rabbinic tradition delineates two types of fear of God: (1) fear of punishment by God; (2) awe at God's grandeur. The concluding verses of Ecclesiastes should be understood in the second sense: we must live a life awed by God's greatness. Feeling the presence of the eternal and infinite God empowers us to live deeper, more meaningful lives. In spite of our mortality, we are able to relate to the immortal Source of all life.

"Keep His commandments": God did impose mitzvoth (commandments) on us not to crush our freedom and autonomy, but rather to give us divine guidance on how best to live our lives. The mitzvoth are basic sources of freedom and spiritual blessings—not heavy, mindless burdens. Maimonides explained that the commandments were given by the all-wise God in order to perfect us. The commandments provide us with aim and focus in life; they enable us to escape the ennui and futility that characterize so much of humanity.

Pirkei Avot 6:2 teaches that no one is as free as those who occupy themselves with Torah. Those who truly experience Torah and mitzvoth are blessed with an incredible inner freedom, autonomy, and meaning in life.

"The whole of man": The Jerusalem Talmud (*Berakhot* 2:8–5c) records words of eulogy given by a great sage upon the passing of Rabbi Levi ben Sisi, another leading rabbi of that generation. The eulogizer noted that Rabbi Levi was uniquely great. He had been able to preserve and transmit the teachings of his teacher Rabbi Yehuda HaNasi as no other sage had been able to do. The eulogy closed with the words of Ecclesiastes: "For this is the whole of man."

I think the eulogizer, reflecting on the greatness of Rabbi Levi ben Sisi, realized that the best that can be said about anyone is that he fulfilled his mission in life. Rabbi Levi had devoted his years to studying and teaching Torah in the tradition of his illustrious teacher, Rabbi Yehuda. He had been eminently successful in his life's work. "This is the whole of man." This is the entire purpose and meaning of life. Yes, death is inevitable; but death does not negate the value of the life one has led. A person who reaches his maximum capacity has achieved something noteworthy, something that transcends death. Such a person is "whole."

"For God will bring every work into the judgment": King Solomon concludes the book of Ecclesiastes with a profound, life-altering truth: whatever we think, whatever we do—we are answerable to God. Life is not random and not meaningless. There is a God who is conscious of our lives and who judges us with a totality of knowledge. We have no secrets before God. God knows, far better than we ourselves know, to what extent we have fulfilled our life's mission and to what extent we have fallen short.

The Talmud (*Shabbat* 31a) speculates on the questions we will be asked by the heavenly court after we have died. These questions reflect the Rabbinic sages' notions of what constitutes a good life. Did we conduct our business affairs with honesty? Did we set aside regular times for Torah study? Did we raise our families properly? Did we yearn for salvation—that is, the messianic era of peace for all humanity? Did we delve into the depths of the Torah's wisdom?

The ultimate questions, as Ecclesiastes teaches, are questions of the quality of our lives—not the quantity of what we have been able to accumulate. The heavenly court will not ask us if we were rich, or powerful, or famous. Rather, it will challenge us to determine if we have lived honestly, thoughtfully, spiritually, morally. Have we plumbed the depths of Torah wisdom? Have we striven to bring the world closer to the messianic ideals?

Divine judgment awaits us at the end of our life's journey. But for us to be ready for that judgment, we need to judge ourselves honestly and truly, "for that is the whole of man."

PART TWO

Wisdom, Morality, and Righteousness

Proverbs/*Mishlei*

The Pursuit of Wisdom

The proverbs of Solomon the son of David, king of Israel;
to know wisdom and instruction; to comprehend the
words of understanding; to receive the discipline of wisdom, justice, right, and equity.

(PROVERBS 1:1–3)

How long, you thoughtless, will you love thoughtlessness? And how long will scorners delight themselves in
scorning and fools hate knowledge?

(PROVERBS 1:22)

Life can be confusing. We might accumulate a wealth of facts but
still not know how to live a proper life. We might have incisive
minds but still miss the larger ideas that shape our world. We might
think we understand human nature but still fall very short of fath-
oming why people act and think the way they do. We may pursue
truth but still find ourselves grappling with illusions.

King Solomon opens the book of Proverbs with a set of instruc-
tions that will enable us to distinguish between truth and falsehood,
to see things as they really are. The goal is not to attain abstract
philosophical truths, but to gain the capacity to live good, moral,
and upright lives.

"To know" means that before setting out on a journey, we need
to know where we are headed and how to get there. An ill-planned
trip may lead to disaster or may end up far from where we had
hoped to arrive. A wise person seeks to know the overarching plan.
The journey is not to be a series of random, haphazard decisions.

Life is to be lived wisely, with a clear focus on how we are to proceed from youth to old age, from birth to death.

"To comprehend" means to be able to make sharp distinctions, to differentiate between the correct route and the tempting detours that lead to dead ends. Life is filled with moral dilemmas, and it is all too easy to make choices based on what seems most pleasant or expedient for the moment. If we cannot make clear distinctions, we risk going off course.

"To receive the discipline of wisdom, justice, right, and equity" means to recognize that wisdom is to be applied in ways that conduce to a moral, decent way of life for ourselves and for society at large. Without self-discipline, we may casually slip into a careless, thoughtless, and selfish way of life.

Crude and scornful people abound. They do not pursue wisdom. They live from moment to moment without overarching ideals. They are not concerned with the larger questions of philosophy, morality, or spirituality. They do not understand that they will ultimately need to give an accounting for their lives.

A rabbinic parable tells of a poor man who was struggling to support his family. He learned of a faraway land that was filled with precious jewels. A ship would soon be leaving for this land, and it had room for him as a passenger. But the ship would return only after an interval of unspecified length. His wife agreed that he should make the voyage, so as to be able to obtain valuable jewels to bring back to support his family in wealth and honor.

So the man boarded the ship and was off to make his fortune. Sure enough, the ship arrived at the faraway land, and it was indeed filled with treasures. The earth was covered with diamonds and all types of precious stones. He hurriedly filled his pockets with jewels; he stuffed his bags with gems. He was now an extraordinarily rich man. He rejoiced in the thought of how wealthy he and his family would be upon his return home.

But in the faraway land, the man soon realized that his precious stones were valueless. They were so abundant that no one paid any attention to them. None of the storekeepers would accept them as payment for merchandise. Rather, the currency of this land was wax candles. Everyone strove to accumulate as many wax candles as possible; their wealth and power were evaluated by the number of candles they possessed.

It did not take long for the man to recognize his need for wax candles. He worked hard to gain as many as he could. Soon, he had accumulated a large number of them. He emptied his pockets and bags of the diamonds, rubies, and emeralds and filled them instead with wax candles. In this new land, he became wealthy and prominent.

Time passed. It was now time for the man to return to his wife and family. The ship was ready to leave. Quickly, the man packed his bags with as many candles as he could possibly carry, and then he boarded the ship.

When he arrived home, his wife eagerly greeted him. She asked to see the treasures he had brought back. Proudly, the man opened his bags and emptied his pockets. He stacked up piles of wax candles. His wife was astonished. "You spent all that time in the faraway land, a land filled with precious jewels, and you brought back only piles of nearly worthless wax candles?"

Suddenly, the man realized he had made a terrible mistake. When he had arrived in the faraway land, he knew he was supposed to gather precious gems—but he had soon forgotten his mission. Influenced by the people in that land, he had come to value candles and ignore jewels. He had thought that by accumulating candles, he had become successful. But now that he had returned home, he realized that he had missed his opportunity to bring back real treasures. Instead of jewels, he came back with a pile of candles.

We are placed on earth to attain transcendent treasures—wisdom, love, spiritual insight, moral courage. If we can keep our lives focused on these goals, we can return to our heavenly home with genuine treasures. But in this world, people chase after "wax candles"—material wealth, fancy cars, glitz, hedonistic lifestyles. In this world, people are judged to be successful by the false standards of materialism and hedonism. It is possible to lose sight of our real treasures and goals, to pursue the values that pervade our society. When we finally return home—to our heavenly home beyond—we may realize that we are bringing with us "wax candles" instead of precious jewels—that we had lived our lives chasing falsehoods and vanities, rather than pursuing goodness, truth, and piety.

King Solomon asked the poignant question: "How long, you thoughtless, will you love thoughtlessness?"

The Wisdom of Our Fathers
and Our Mothers

Hear, my son, the instruction of your father, and forsake
not the teaching of your mother.

(PROVERBS 1:8)

Rabbi Joseph B. Soloveitchik credited the community of Jews committed to the *masorah* (the traditional Jewish way of life) as the
group who ensured Jewish survival over the millennia. According to
Soloveitchik, the *masorah* community was founded by Moses and
will continue into messianic times. It includes those Jews for whom
Torah study and observance are the central features of life:

> The *masorah* community cuts across the centuries, indeed
> millennia, of calendaric time and unites those who already
> played their part, delivered their message, acquired fame,
> and withdrew from the covenantal stage quietly and hum-
> bly, with those who have not yet been given the opportu-
> nity to appear on the covenantal stage and who wait for
> their turn in the anonymity of the "about to be."[1]

The *masorah* community has sacrificed mightily over the millennia
so that the ideals and values of Torah could be passed on from generation to generation. Without that unflinching devotion, the chain
of tradition weakens and breaks.

Rabbi Soloveitchik notes that the *masorah* community embod-
ies two dimensions, that of the fathers and that of the mothers. In
expounding on this thought, he draws on his personal experience:

> The laws of Shabbat, for instance, were passed on to me
> by my father; they are part of "the instruction of your

77

father." The Shabbat as a living entity, as a queen, was revealed to me by my mother; it is part of the "teaching of your mother." The fathers *knew* much about the Shabbat; the mothers *lived* the Shabbat, experienced her presence, and perceived her beauty and splendor. The fathers taught generations how to observe the Shabbat; mothers taught generations how to greet the Shabbat and how to enjoy her twenty-four hour presence.[2]

Judaism has depended on the harmonious blending of these two prototypical models. The fathers conveyed content, explained the laws, maintained discipline. The mothers provided the warmth and beauty of the tradition. Giving heed only to the fathers results in a formalistic, overintellectualized religious life; observing only the teachings of the mothers results in a shallow, feel-good way of life that lacks content. Together, the "fathers" and the "mothers" provide us with wholeness.

Thousands of years ago, the wise King Solomon understood that transmission of tradition depends equally on the fathers and the mothers of each generation. He reminds the children to pay close attention to both parents, since each has a unique message and style. The fathers and mothers not only provide us with our physical lives; they also are charged with laying the foundations for our spiritual lives.

Righteousness Beyond
the Letter of the Law

That you may walk in the way of good men and keep the
paths of the righteous.

(PROVERBS 2:20)

So shall you find grace and good favor in the sight of God
and man.

(PROVERBS 3:4)

In all your ways know Him, and He will direct your paths.

(PROVERBS 3:6)

The spirit of man is the lamp of the Lord, searching all the
inward parts.

(PROVERBS 20:27)

The Talmud (*Bava Metzia* 83a) relates that porters working for
Rabba bar Bar Hana carelessly broke a barrel of his wine. To recoup
his loss, Rabba bar Bar Hana seized the porters' coats as pledges
until they paid him for the damage they had caused. The workers
protested and called him to judgment before the great sage Rav.
Rav ordered that the coats be returned to the workers.

"Is that the law?" asked the surprised Rabba bar Bar Hana.

"Yes," said Rav, "for it is written [Proverbs 2:20], 'That you may
walk in the way of good men.'"

Rabba bar Bar Hana returned the coats to the porters, but the porters were still not satisfied. "We worked all day but have not been paid!" Rav ordered that the workers be paid for their labor, even though they had obviously not done a good job.

Rabba bar Bar Hana was astounded. "Is that the law?" he asked.

Rav replied, "Yes, because the verse also states, 'Keep the paths of the righteous.'"

Rav insisted that the law itself demanded going beyond the technical letter of the law; it included the moral responsibility of behaving in a good and compassionate way. Business is not an abstract, neutral forum but a domain of interrelationships among human beings. These interrelationships must reflect humaneness. We must be willing to forgo our rights for the sake of being good and righteous. The Talmud (*Bava Metzia* 30b) records the opinion of Rabbi Yohanan: "Jerusalem was destroyed because people insisted on enforcing their legal rights." When society becomes a battleground of claims and counterclaims, when each person seeks the advantage even at the cost of ruining others—then the society has become corrupt, even if everything is done according to the law.

Yes, societies need to function with a proper legal system, and yes, not everyone will be willing to forgo his or her rights in every case. Yet, each individual has the power to rise above the letter of the law and to live on a higher level.

The Talmud (*Sanhedrin* 6b) offers an example of how King David would balance the sometimes conflicting claims of justice and compassion. If a case came before him that involved a wealthy and a poor man and strict justice was in favor of the wealthy man, then King David would rule justly and declare in favor of the rich party. But then David himself would pay the wealthy man whatever the poor man would have been obligated to pay! Thus he upheld both justice and compassion. Not every judge is as wealthy as King David, but the Talmud is citing this case as an ideal. The law must be just, but the quality of compassion must not be abandoned in the process.

Pirkei Avot 5:14 cites the opinion that if one says "what's mine is mine and what's yours is yours," this reflects the attitude of the wicked people of Sodom. On the surface, this attitude does not seem to be wicked at all. It merely states what many believe: I've worked for what I have, and it is all mine; you are not my responsibility. You keep what you earn, and you have no obligation to share with me. Yet, at root this is the characteristic of Sodom. It fosters a worldview centered on the self, seeing each person as an independent island. It does not acknowledge the moral interrelatedness of human beings.

King Solomon reminded us that we are answerable to a higher authority, that our conduct must seek to find favor in the sight of God and human beings. If we feel the presence of God in our daily lives and actions, we will strive to be better than merely clinging to the letter of the law. We will want to be righteous; we will want to be concerned for the feelings and needs of others. God knows our inner thoughts and intentions.

We Are Caretakers, Not Owners

Honor the Lord with your substance, and with the first-
fruits of all your increase.

(PROVERBS 3:9)

The sages of Talmudic times often expressed profound ideas in
terse, enigmatic statements. An example of this is found in the
midrashic comment "The world was created in the merit of three
things: in the merit of [the mitzvoth of] *hallah*, tithes, and first
fruits" (*Yalkut Shimoni*, Genesis 1:2). If we were to speculate as to
which mitzvoth were absolutely vital to the creation of the universe,
we might have chosen other—seemingly more important—commandments, such as the Sabbath, the laws of holiness, the worship
of one God, and so on.

What did the author of this midrash have in mind? Why did he
think that the laws of *hallah*, tithes, and first fruits were so vital to
the creation of the world? To answer these questions, we need to
ponder the significance of these three mitzvoth.

All three of these commandments are reminders that we ultimately own nothing and that the universe belongs to God. God
allows us to be guardians and caretakers of property, and we are
expected to uphold our responsibilities faithfully. When we make a
batch of dough, we take off a piece as *hallah*. In Temple days, this
was given as a gift to the priests in the Temple. Today, with the
absence of the Temple in Jerusalem, we burn a bit of dough as a
reminder that it is not ours. We may not use the rest of the dough
until we've first taken out the *hallah*.

A farmer works hard to bring in a crop. He might think: this all
belongs to me; I've done the labor; I've invested time and money:
the produce is all mine. The Torah reminds us: No, it is not yours,

it is God's. One-tenth must be given to the Levites; a tenth of the remainder must be given to the poor or must be brought to Jerusalem to be eaten there.

A farmer sees the first fruits budding on his trees; he has worked long and hard to earn the harvest. Yet, he must designate the very first fruits as an offering to the Almighty.

These three mitzvoth underscore the vital fact that the world was created by and belongs to God. We are transient guests here. The Almighty blesses us with property to sustain ourselves and our families—but it is ours only insofar as God enjoins us to be worthy caretakers.

These three mitzvoth point to the ultimate truth—well beyond the realm of agriculture—that all our property and assets are on temporary loan to us from the Almighty. This is not merely an abstract idea but is a foundation for a wise philosophy of life. If we think that what we earn is all ours and only ours, we are sadly mistaken; it is ours only by virtue of the fact that God has allowed us to have it on loan. We literally cannot take it with us. These three commandments epitomize our sense of gratitude to the Almighty for what God gives us. They teach us humility and charity. They put life into a spiritual perspective.

We work hard to earn income, to invest wisely, to enjoy our worldly assets. When we understand on the profoundest level that all our material assets are simply temporary loans from God, we can live more responsibly and more wisely. By setting aside part of our material wealth to help the needy and to support charitable institutions, we thereby demonstrate our recognition of God as Master of the universe. Tithing and giving charity are not merely acts of kindness; they are fulfillments of practical obligations that God has placed on us. The midrashic sage who taught that the world was created in the merit of the mitzvoth of *hallah*, tithes, and first fruits was pointing to a deep truth that is at the foundation of a righteous, moral life.[1]

Resilience When Facing Adversity

For whom the Lord loves He corrects, even as a father
[corrects] the son in whom he delights.

(PROVERBS 3:12)

For the commandment is a lamp and the teaching is light,
and reproofs of instruction are the way of life.

(PROVERBS 6:23)

If you faint in the day of adversity, your strength is small
indeed.

(PROVERBS 24:10)

For a righteous man falls seven times and rises up again;
but the wicked stumble under adversity.

(PROVERBS 24:16)

It is impossible to get through life without facing difficult times—
illness, death of loved ones, emotional anguish, financial setbacks.
The Psalmist beseeches God, "Give us joy as the days You have
afflicted us" (Psalm 90:15). Apparently, we are to be considered fortunate if our good days equal our days of affliction. If we have many
more good days, we are indeed blessed.

The Talmud (*Taanit* 21a) tells of a pious Jew by the name of
Nahum Ish Gamzo. He was given this epithet because his motto
was *Gam zo letovah*, "This also is for the best." No matter how
much he suffered—and he suffered a great deal—he took it in

stride. He had faith that his sufferings were chastisements of love from the Almighty. Whatever God willed was for the best.

Another Talmudic passage (*Berakhot* 5a) tells of a great sage who did not look favorably upon his sufferings. He wanted relief from his pain and did not share Nahum Ish Gamzo's attitude of acceptance of sufferings.

Sufferings are normal aspects of being human; sickness, accidents, loss, and alienation are facts of life. However, we sometimes may feel that our sufferings are punishments or chastisements from the Almighty. We are called upon to examine our ways and to repent for past errors.

Some people are crushed by setbacks. Others face crisis with great faith and courage. King Solomon suggests that we can better face our inevitable troubles if we put our lives in a spiritual perspective. If we see our sufferings as wake-up calls from God, we might draw on inner strength that we did not even realize we had.

Dr. James Hall, a prominent psychiatrist and author from Dallas, Texas, suffered a terrible stroke in the early 1990s, leaving him a quadriplegic. He was no longer able to maintain his active, vibrant, and high-powered life. His physical condition left him in a state of relative helplessness. A computer keyboard was specially devised to enable him to communicate.

Facing this horrible challenge, Dr. Hall rethought the meaning of his life. He wrote:

> Life is, if anything, more interesting than before I was disabled. I don't worry now about such things as reputation and earning a living. With essentially nothing to lose, I am more open about what I think.[1]

Shortly before his stroke, he had a vivid dream, which now seemed prescient. In his dream, an authoritative voice called out to him, "You are not leading your true life."[2] Now, as a quadriplegic, he felt the need to respond to that voice; he needed to understand how to lead his true life. Although Dr. Hall would never have chosen to be stricken with a devastating stroke, he found that it enabled him to find meaning, strength, and redemption that he otherwise would never have known.

Sufferings and setbacks, in spite of their negative features, can be taken as tests of our personal strength. It is as though the Almighty is challenging us to correctly assess our resilience so that we may emerge with greater clarity.

An article in *Time* magazine reported on research dealing with resilience, the ability to deal with difficult challenges. Among the findings is that people can train their minds to cope better when they are confronted with fear and with disaster.

> New research shows humans can train their brains to build and strengthen different connections that don't reinforce the fear circuit [in the brain]. Over time, if people use this new pathway enough, it can become the new response to stress.[3]

Individuals who receive training in "mindfulness"—in paying close attention to what they are doing—develop greater resilience. They cope better with crises, and they recover more quickly from duress. Those who practice meditation, for example, can transform how their brain reacts to crisis. They develop quietude and resilience, helping them to decrease or overcome panic, fear, or despair.

Suffering, pain, and loss are inevitable features of life. While we might not be readily able to say that "these too are for the best," we can learn from these challenges. We might even achieve greater insight into the meaning of our lives and our relationship with others. Resilience may not enable us to get over our losses, but it will help us get through them.

Rabbi Adin Steinsaltz has noted, "The ability to persist, to continue, is what distinguishes one person from another and, on a larger scale, between one people and another."[4] Setbacks are normal features of life. The important thing is to have the fortitude to recover, reenergize, and rediscover the strengths we may not even know that we had.

Religion at Its Best ... and Worst

Her ways are ways of pleasantness, and all her paths are
peace. She is a tree of life to them that lay hold upon her,
and happy is everyone who holds her fast.

(PROVERBS 3:17–18)

Religion has two faces. One face is that of saintliness, idealism, holiness, and selflessness. But the other face is one of hatred, cruelty, selfishness, and egotism. Within the world of religion, we can find the most exemplary human beings, but we can also find inquisitors and terrorists. In his play *The Father*, August Strindberg has one of his characters state, "It is strange that as soon as you begin to talk about God and love, your voice becomes hard and your eyes full of hate."

According to a Rabbinic homily, Mount Sinai was chosen for God's revelation because it is a low, humble mountain. God wanted the recipients of Torah to appreciate the value of humility and to avoid the vice of arrogance. A Talmudic passage (*Shabbat* 89a–b) links the word *Sinai* with the word *sinah*—hatred. Those who emulate the ideals of Sinai are those who reflect the beautiful face of religion. Those who breach those ideals fall into the trap of *sinah*, becoming hateful and jealous. There is a fine line between Sinai and *sinah*. Alexander Solzhenitsyn has pointed out that "the line dividing good and evil acts through the heart of every human being. And who is willing to destroy a piece of his own heart?"[1]

The ways of Torah are ways of pleasantness and peace. Hateful, rude, and hostile ways are by definition antithetical to the true teachings of religion and morality.

A *New York Times* article by Professor Adam Grant, "Raising a Moral Child," also sheds light on the Sinai/*sinah* dichotomy.[2]

Professor Grant notes that when disciplining a child, a parent should be careful to criticize the child's actions, not the child him- or herself. For example, we should not say, "You are a bad boy/ girl"; rather we should say, "You behaved badly." We should not say, "You are foolish," but rather, "You acted foolishly." What is the difference?

When a parent says that a child is bad/foolish/stubborn, the child internalizes that indeed he is in essence bad, foolish, or stubborn. When a parent says that the child's behavior was unacceptable, then the lesson is: you are good, but your actions need correction. The child's self-respect is maintained, and she knows that she can improve. The child is not stigmatized by a negative self-image of being bad, foolish, or stubborn by nature. A Sinai approach is to criticize faulty behavior, in the hope of generating better behavior from the child in the future. A *sinah* approach tears down the child's ego.

This lesson applies not only to children. When criticizing others—including adults—we should not call names or give negative labels. Rather, we should address the problematic action or idea without casting aspersion on the basic goodness of the person being criticized.[3]

The way of the Torah is the path of pleasantness, kindness, and compassion. Veering from that path is destructive to our self, our society, and our religion.

Who We Are and Who We Can Be

There are six things that the Lord hates, and seven that are an abomination unto Him: haughty eyes, a lying tongue, and hands that shed innocent blood; a heart that devises wicked thoughts, feet that are swift in running to evil; a false witness who breathes out lies, and he who sows discord among brethren.

(PROVERBS 6:16–19)

Stolen waters are sweet, and bread eaten in secret is pleasant.

(PROVERBS 9:17)

The Kotzker Rebbe (1787–1859) was an important Hasidic leader known for his incisive mind and his impatience with human frailties. He was once told by his personal secretary that some of the rebbe's silverware had been stolen. The Kotzker cried out in disbelief, "Stolen? Is it not written in the Torah, 'You shall not steal'?" To him, it was unthinkable that anyone would willingly violate an ethical commandment of the Torah.

And yet, his silverware indeed had been stolen. People did—and do—sin. They may know in theory that God hates arrogance, lies, murder, wickedness, theft, troublemaking; and yet they do these things anyway. Why?

People commit abominable acts for a variety of motives. They may be seeking personal gain, or taking vengeance, or trying to assert their own personal power over others; or they may be mentally ill or psychologically damaged. It seems to be a fact of human life that society has a significant number of people who are outright criminals; it also includes a great many who behave immorally but are never arrested for their crimes.

King Solomon reminds us that "stolen waters are sweet, and bread eaten in secret is pleasant." People derive a certain degree of pleasure in doing that which is forbidden. Perhaps this provides a sense of freedom and power; perhaps this lets us think that we have outsmarted the system. Since the days of Adam and Eve, humans have been confronted with temptations, and since the days of Adam and Eve, humans have succumbed to temptations.

Each human being has the capacity to be righteous, and each has the capacity to be wicked. Each has the responsibility to shape the direction of his life; each can make her life an achievement of greatness or a monument of ugly failure.

In Hebrew, the usual word for sin is *het*. At its root, the word *het* means "missing the mark." The assumption is that people are aiming to behave honestly and morally, but they may veer off course. Their goal is to be upright and fine human beings, but due to errors in judgment or self-control, the goal is missed. They give in to the temptation to sin.

The Torah reports on an amazing dream of our forefather Jacob. He had fled from his brother Esau's wrath and was on his way to Laban, his future father-in-law. At nightfall, Jacob went to sleep. "And he dreamed, and behold a ladder set up on the earth, and the top of it reached to heaven; and behold, the angels of God were ascending and descending on it" (Genesis 28:12). The usual understanding of this verse is that the angels were ascending and descending the rungs of the ladder.

A midrash (*Genesis Rabbah* 28:12) offers a different explanation. The Hebrew words *olim veyordim bo* (ascending and descending on it) can also be translated "ascending and descending on *him*." That is, the angels were jumping up and down on Jacob himself! The angels said to him, "'Are you the one whose image is engraved on high?' They ascended on high and saw his [ideal] image and they descended below and found him sleeping." According to this midrash, the ideal image of Jacob was in heaven near the throne of the glory of God. That ideal image represents the person Jacob

could become ... and should become. The angels viewed this per-
fected image of Jacob in heaven but then descended to earth and
found the sleeping Jacob, who seemed unaware or unconcerned
about his heavenly self. The angels pounced on him, as if to say,
"Wake up—don't you realize who you can become, who you are
supposed to become?"

This midrash relates not only to Jacob but to all human beings.
In a sense, we each are two people: our heavenly ideal self and our
earthly self. The heavenly self is an ideal to which we should aspire.
We are each born with unique talents, sensitivities, opportunities. If
we strive to develop ourselves to our maximum potential, we can
approach the heavenly ideal of ourselves. We will realize that the
"stolen waters" may taste sweet in the short run but that they are
poisonous to our moral development in the long run.

What Do We Remember about the Righteous?

The memory of the righteous shall be for a blessing; but the name of the wicked shall rot.

(PROVERBS 10:7)

In his book *Being Mortal*, Dr. Atul Gawande teaches that living a meaningful life goes beyond simply providing for our physical needs. Most human beings are not content with looking out for their own self-interest without regard for anyone else.

> Consider the fact that we care deeply about what happens to the world after we die.... The only way death is not meaningless is to see yourself as part of something greater: a family, a community, a society. If you don't, mortality is only a horror.[1]

Dr. Gawande cites Josiah Royce, a Harvard philosopher who wrote *The Philosophy of Loyalty* (1908). Dr. Royce understood loyalty as a commitment to a cause beyond ourselves. Whereas an individualist puts personal needs first, the loyal person is prepared for self-sacrifice on behalf of loved ones or a noble cause. Royce believed that loyalty

> solves the paradox of our ordinary existence by showing us outside of ourselves the cause which is to be served, and inside of ourselves the will which delights to do this service, and which is not thwarted but enriched and expressed in such service.[2]

Put more simply, loyal people live for something beyond themselves; serving that cause—a loved one, society, one's country—is a source of delight and personal gratification. This is what gives meaning to our lives.

Think of four or five individuals you have known whom you would describe as being righteous. These individuals may not be perfect in every way, but they have significant qualities that have earned your admiration. What are those qualities? Humility, wisdom, dedication, willingness to sacrifice self for the sake of others, courage ... the list goes on. But some qualities that you would not ascribe to a righteous person are arrogance, rudeness, selfishness, willingness to hurt others for the sake of personal gain, moral turpitude. When we think of righteous people, we feel uplifted and inspired; remembering them is a blessing. When we think of unrighteous people, we feel sullied and disgusted; remembering them is no blessing.

King Solomon writes that "the memory of the righteous shall be for a blessing." Why didn't he simply state that the righteous person is a blessing? Why speak of "the memory" of such a person?

While it is certainly a blessing to be in the presence of a righteous person, we often do not fully appreciate that person until he has died! In my forty-six years in the rabbinate, I have officiated at a great many funerals and have visited numerous houses of mourning. Often I have heard people—including those who were closest to the deceased—lament that they did not fully appreciate the one who had died. They didn't realize how truly good she was, how he did so much for so many but was not fully recognized for his kindnesses. As the survivors reminisce, they are surprised by how much they did not know about the deceased! Many of her sacrifices were made quietly and had not been noticed at the time. Many of his good deeds were done without fanfare, without anyone fully realizing his selflessness. Now, after we have lost this person, we become aware of qualities and actions that we did not fully understand during her lifetime. The "memory of the righteous shall be for a blessing."

No Secrets from God

He who walks uprightly walks securely; but he who per-
verts his ways shall be found out.

(PROVERBS 10:9)

When the great sage Rabban Yohanan ben Zakkai (first century CE)
was nearing death, his students asked him for some parting words of
wisdom. He replied, "May your fear of heaven be as great as your
fear of humans" (Talmud, *Berakhot* 28b). The students were perplexed. Was this the greatest blessing he could offer them?

Rabban Yohanan ben Zakkai was pointing to an important truth.
When people wish to sin, they look around to see if any humans
are looking. If no one is around, they feel safe in proceeding with
their plans. They don't seem to be concerned that God is watching.
They fear detection by human beings but don't fear the watchful-
ness of the Almighty. Rabban Yohanan was teaching that one's fear
of heaven—that is, awareness of the presence of God—should be at
least as great as one's fear of being seen by human beings.

People behave unethically. They cheat, they steal, they lie, and
they even murder. More often than not, they find ways to justify
their behavior. They imagine that they might be able to get away
with their crimes or sins without ever being detected. But more
often than not, they are found out. Even if others never discover
their misdeeds, they themselves know what they have done. Sometimes this self-knowledge is the greatest punishment; it never lets
them rest—they are always afraid of being unmasked.

In his play *All My Sons*, Arthur Miller depicts the life and death
of Joe Keller. He and his partner manufactured airplane engines.
During the war, the government ordered many engines, and the
company flourished. But a serious flaw was discovered; the engines

94

were not safe. The company sold the damaged engines anyway, and a number of pilots lost their lives flying defective aircraft. An investigation was conducted, and Keller's partner was sent to prison. Keller himself claimed to have no knowledge of the sale of defective engines. He went on to live a seemingly comfortable life.

But in the end, he could not conceal his complicity in the crime. His son demanded the truth. Keller had not only made money selling flawed merchandise, he had manipulated things so that his partner shouldered all the blame. Keller tried to justify himself:

> I'm in business, a man is in business; a hundred and twenty [engines] cracked, you're out of business; you got a process, the process don't work you're out of business; you don't know how to operate, your stuff is no good; they close you up, they tear up your contracts, what the hell's it to them? You lay forty years into a business and they knock you out in five minutes, what could I do, let them take forty years, let them take my life away?[1]

Once the family understood the complicity of Joe Keller in this immoral sale of cracked airplane engines, his life came apart. He could no longer face them—or himself. Suicide was his way out.

Arthur Miller's play reflected real-life situations. During the American mobilization for World War II, it was found that a number of manufacturers were supplying faulty military equipment to the government. A Senate commission, under the chairmanship of Senator Harry S. Truman, conducted investigations. The manufacturer of the B-26 bomber admitted that the wings of the aircraft had not been built correctly and posed a serious threat to pilots of those planes. When Truman asked why the design for the wings had not been corrected, the manufacturer said that plans were too advanced to make changes. It would take too much time and cost too much money. The Truman commission also inquired about a newly constructed tanker that broke in two. The manufacturers had used substandard steel plate but had charged the government for the higher-grade steel that had been ordered. A spokesman for the company admitted a "misrepresentation" but denied that the inferior steel posed a problem to the ship. Yet, the ship came apart! The Truman commission interviewed highly important business leaders who knew they were making decisions that would jeopardize the lives of American military personnel but made these decisions because they could make more money for themselves and their companies.[2]

These business leaders, like Joe Keller, thought that business is business, that making profit was more important than worrying about possible danger to others. People in many businesses do the same thing. They sell dangerous drugs, tainted food, or defective products. People behave immorally and foolishly in ways that damage others and damage themselves. They take bribes and kickbacks; they engage in illegal business dealings. They pay no heed to the advice of Rabban Yohanan ben Zakkai; they hope to avoid human detection but do not realize that they are being watched by the Almighty. They will have to answer for their behavior, if not in this world, then in the world-to-come.

Rabbi Yehuda HaNasi, compiler of the Mishnah, taught, "Reflect on three things and you will not fall into transgression: Know what is above you: a seeing eye, a hearing ear, and a book in which all your deeds are written" (*Pirkei Avot* 2:1).

When We Are Betrayed

A false balance is an abomination to the Lord; but a perfect weight is His delight.

(PROVERBS 11:1)

We go to a food store and fill our shopping carts. We go to the
cashier and pay. The cashier weighs the items that need to be
weighed and tells us how much we owe. We pay and leave the store
with our purchases.

Sometime later, we learn that we had been cheated. The store's
scales were calibrated so that everything appeared to weigh more
than it actually did. We bought five pounds of almonds, but the
scale recorded five and a half pounds. It was not a huge margin of
error, but the result was that we—and all other customers—had
been overcharged. It is a moral responsibility of the storekeeper to
ensure that the scales are working properly.

If we learn that the storekeeper had intentionally set the scales
so as to increase the weight of the merchandise that was placed on
it, we would feel betrayed. We had trusted a person to deal with
us fairly and honestly, and that person has violated our trust. Even
if that storekeeper were to give us a full refund, we would still feel
deep sorrow. It would be very difficult for that storekeeper to regain
our trust.

King Solomon puts our everyday business dealings into a religious context. Not only are we disgusted by false scales, God
also finds these scales to be an abomination. Not only are we
pleased when people conduct themselves honestly, but God also
is delighted. This is a strong way of saying that our business conduct matters not only to ourselves and to our customers, but to the
Almighty.

A story is told of a dairyman in a small village who used to provide milk to the local population. In order to increase his profits, he
decided to dilute the milk with 5 percent water. People seemed not
to notice the difference, so a few months later he added 5 percent
more water. Again, he received no complaints ... so he continued to
dilute the milk, little by little, month after month. People paid full
price for diluted milk, and the milkman was making a nice profit.

After a while, though, the dairyman felt remorse at his own wickedness. He was literally stealing money from his customers by selling them diluted milk for the price of whole milk. In a spirit of
repentance, he decided to stop diluting the milk. But no sooner
had he begun to sell whole milk, his customers started to complain
angrily. They accused the milkman of altering the milk, of trying to
cheat them. The milk no longer tasted the same!

The milkman went to his rabbi in desperation. He told the full
story of how he had deceived his customers for many months by
diluting the milk. But now that he had repented and was selling
milk at its full strength, people were accusing him of cheating
them. They had grown accustomed to diluted milk. The real milk
now tasted bad to them. The dairyman asked the rabbi what he
should do.

The rabbi thought: To sell diluted milk is a sin. To sell whole
milk arouses anger and accusations on the part of the customers.
So the rabbi advised: Just as you diluted the milk gradually so that
people got used to the dilution, so you should gradually lessen the
dilution until people get used to whole milk again. Whatever profit
you make from the dilutions, you must contribute to charity and
not keep even one cent of immoral profit for yourself.

This story is relevant not just for dairy farmers, but for nations,
for institutions, for each individual. It is easy to dilute principles and
ideals for the sake of apparent gains. As long as people feel they can
get away with lower standards, they keep sacrificing a bit more, and
then a bit more. They gradually lose integrity and authenticity. If or
when they wake up and realize how far they have sold out their own
souls, they have trouble figuring out how to return to their original
standard. People have become used to their current diluted manner

of behavior and may react badly if they suddenly stand up for their old principles again. It takes time to gradually regain one's own sense of balance and to regain the confidence and trust of others.

To ensure our authenticity and integrity, we need to know what our standards and ideals are; we need to have the clarity and character to avoid diluting or betraying ourselves. We need to be aware of our strengths and weaknesses and to be able to avoid diluting ourselves for the sake of attaining dubious social or economic gains.

Bringing milk back to full strength is a challenge. A greater challenge is to make sure that we ourselves are living honestly and at full strength.[1]

What Is Humility?

When pride comes, then comes shame; but with the humble is wisdom.

(PROVERBS 11:2)

When we use the word "humane," we generally think of the qualities of kindness, empathy, and compassion. When we say that someone's behavior is "inhumane," we generally mean that the person has acted viciously, remorselessly.

We commonly contrast "humane" and "beastly" behavior. Whereas humans care for each other's well-being, beasts are driven by survival-of-the-fittest instincts. They kill in order to eat. They kill to protect their turf. Humans are altruistic and self-sacrificing; animals will do whatever is necessary to ensure their own survival. Even if beasts sometimes display altruism, the general rule is otherwise.

The etymological root of "human" and "humane" is the Latin word *humus*, "earth." To be human is to be conscious of our earthiness. The Bible had long ago taught that God fashioned humans from the dust of the earth; from dust we were created, and to dust we will return. This recognition of our earthy existence should make us humble. "Humble" also derives from the root meaning "earth." The distinctive characteristic of being human is being humble.

People often equate humility with passivity and self-effacement. But that is not the true meaning of humility. A humble person is someone who is fully conscious of her earthiness. Recognizing the lowliness, transience, and frailty of life, a humble person strives to be kind, compassionate, and empathetic. She does not live only to advance herself but seeks to play a role in creating a good family and society. After all, we are all mortal, and we will be passing through our lives soon enough. We empathize with fellow human beings, since they—like us—are mortal, frail, and frightened beings.

The Bible describes Moses as being more humble than any other human being. Certainly Moses was not passive or lacking in courage. On the contrary, he was a powerful and dynamic leader who led his people out of slavery. Moses's humility consisted in the fact that he—more than any other human being—was thoroughly aware of his humanity, his mortality, his essential earthiness. Of all humans, Moses alone spoke to God "face to face." The closer we come to the Eternal, the more conscious we are of our mortality. The more we confront the Omnipotent, the more we recognize our own massive limitations. This knowledge does not undermine our sense of self; it strengthens it. It allows us to be realistic about our strengths and weaknesses. To know that we are only "dust and ashes" is the key to living a wise life.

We are more humane as we live humbly. We are more beastly when we behave arrogantly.

What is the basis of arrogance? It is the belief that my survival and success take precedence to that of others. Many human beings, in fact, do not act humanely. They see themselves as being in a competition with others, a competition that they will try to win at whatever cost. They will cheat, lie, or physically harm anyone who gets in their way. The price they pay is the loss of their basic humanity; they come to resemble beasts.

Although the humble may have wisdom, the arrogant often seem to come out ahead in the battle of life. Yet, ultimately the arrogant are shamed; they will answer for their arrogance either in this world or the next.

The late philosopher Dr. Eliezer Berkovitz once posed an agonizing question: if you were given the choice of being a Nazi murderer or an innocent victim murdered by the Nazis, which would you choose? Surely, no decent human being would want to be a Nazi murderer, and no one would choose to be murdered. But what if these were the only two choices available to us?

Dr. Berkovitz concluded that it would be morally preferable to be an innocent victim of murder rather than to be a murderer of innocents. The innocent victim dies with the dignity of a full human being. The Nazi murderer has become a beast, has forfeited his humanity. On the surface it appears that the murderer has won and the victim has lost. In reality, precisely the opposite has happened. The victim has successfully lived and died as a full human being; the murderer has utterly failed to be humane.[1]

The Individual and Society

He who walks with wise men shall be wise; but the companion of fools will worsen.

(PROVERBS 13:20)

There are friends who one has to his own hurt; but there is a friend that sticks closer than a brother.

(PROVERBS 18:24)

Human beings live within a social context. It has been pointed out that second to the death penalty, solitary confinement is the most extreme punishment that can be inflicted on a person. Without social support, we feel lost and depressed; our health deteriorates. Loneliness is one of the most painful experiences to endure.

The social support we receive from birth onward plays a vital role in how we live our lives. Growing up in a healthy, nurturing family is a big plus. Attending good schools, studying with fine teachers, and associating with excellent students are wonderful assets. Being part of a moral, idealistic community is yet another valuable impetus toward leading a good life.

Not everyone grows up with these advantages, and not everyone who begins life with so many pluses actually ends up living a good, happy life. While much of our early life is greatly influenced by our parents, families, and schools, how we ultimately turn out is largely dependent on the choices we ourselves make.

Within each person is a desire to be unique and independent. But there is also an overwhelming desire to conform, to blend in with the group. Monty Python spoofs this tendency in his film

103

Life of Brian where the "Messiah" tells hordes of followers that they don't need him. "You are all individuals," he shouts. And the huge crowd, all dressed alike, reply in unison, "Yes, we are all individuals."

Elias Canetti in his landmark book *Crowds and Power* explores the psychological and sociological factors that lead people to become part of a crowd.[1] Individuals gain a feeling of strength when they merge into a large group of people. Within the crowd, participants feel equality with the others in the group. They gain a feeling of importance, a growing power.

Canetti describes a certain type of crowd that is evident among sports fans. A crowd gathers at a stadium or an arena. The fans enthusiastically root for their teams. Fans feel, in some way, that they are part of their teams; they participate emotionally and vicariously in all of the actions on the playing field. During the game, all fans feel equal, they cheer in unison, and they lose themselves in the excitement of the event. When the game concludes, they shout that "we won" or complain that "we lost" as though they themselves had been playing. Members of the crowd conform to what is expected of fans.

When fans leave the stadium or arena, they return to their usual lives. But in fact they continue to function in the context of other crowds. They find themselves conforming to the behaviors of their families, of their religious communities, of their professional peers. Even when they think they are expressing their individuality, they often do so in a conformist manner like the students in the cartoon *Life of Brian* who profess to be individualists.

To maintain true autonomy, we must be quite strong and clearly focused. We must be able to function within crowds while at the same time holding fast to our true individuality. But how can we best achieve this goal?

The first task is to clarify our own values, our own sense of who we are and who we want to be. The next task is to ensure that we associate with others who most closely fulfill our personal ideals. If we are to be part of a crowd, we need to be sure that it is a crowd composed of fine, moral, courageous people. We need to eschew the temptation to be part of a crowd composed of people whose values we deplore and whose character is morally deficient.

King Solomon pointed to the basic truth: we are deeply influenced by the people around us. We have the power to choose our friends. We have the ability to choose the community in which we live. If we are to fulfill our own potentialities, we will better succeed if we live among wise, kind, and moral people. To spend our lives among fools, deceivers, and criminals is a sure way to drag ourselves down.

Transmitting Culture from Generation to Generation

He who spares his rod hates his son; but he who loves him offers discipline.

(PROVERBS 13:24)

Train a child in the way he should go, and even when he is old he will not depart from it.

(PROVERBS 22:6)

Civilization depends on the effective transmission of knowledge and values from generation to generation. When parents and schools function optimally, children learn the skills and behaviors that will help them lead good lives. But many challenges arise when raising the younger generation. Not all parents and schools are optimal, and neither are all children.

The anthropologist Margaret Mead delineates various types of cultural patterns in her book *Culture and Commitment*.[1] In "postfigurative" societies, the culture was governed by its traditions, and the elders were the authoritative guardians of the traditions. Children were told what to do and when to do it. They grew up in stable communities, and it could be fairly predicted how their lives would turn out. Boys would grow up to work in their father's trade; girls would grow up to become wives and mothers. All would know their place in the society's hierarchy, and there was little mobility and little opportunity for radical change. Some postfigurative cultures still exist in premodern societies. Vestiges of these cultures can still be found among various groups living in the modern world.

These cultures stress the preservation of tradition, veneration of elders, and social stability.

Margaret Mead writes at length about what she calls "cofigurative" cultures. These are societies where the elders have lost much of their authority and where the younger generation is more likely to look for guidance from their peers. A classic example of a cofigurative society is the generation of children of immigrants. For the children, their parents/grandparents represent the "old world." They think and act in ways that are "old-fashioned." They speak the language of their new country with foreign accents. The new generation wants to blend in to the new country. The elders not only cannot give proper advice about the new situation, they might even be seen as an embarrassing handicap to the younger generation. So the new generation turns to its peers in school to learn how to flourish in the new country.

Some elders toss up their hands and give up. They know that their young ones will need to find their own ways and that the elders and their traditions will need to give way. Other elders try to compel their children to follow the old ways, but this generally leads to dissension and rebellion. Yet other elders realize that their wisdom is no longer fully appreciated, but they try to pass on as much of the traditional teachings and values as they can.

At some point, though, the children of cofigurative cultures may come to realize that their peers were not the best teachers after all. Although the elders were "old-fashioned," some of their truths and traditions were actually very beautiful and meaningful. But time has passed, and the world of the elders cannot be retrieved. And yet the peers did not have a better way to cope with the challenges of life. They were shallow, or conformist, or bad mannered.

Margaret Mead then describes another culture, which she calls "prefigurative." This is a culture in which the elders and the youngers are equally pioneers in a new adventure. The elders have lost their traditional authority; the peers have lost their authority; everyone is equally at a loss! Mead thinks that modern Western society is largely in this prefigurative stage. Things change so quickly that it is difficult to stay ahead of the curve. Traditional patterns of family, community, and employment are in flux. Social mobility is a feature of modern life. Young people leave home to attend schools or find employment in other towns. Families disperse; neighborhoods change; traditions weaken or are left behind.

In a prefigurative world, many may feel a bit like Pip in the scene in *Moby Dick* described in the first pages of this book. They lose their moorings; they are not sure who they are or where they are going. Margaret Mead suggests that a prefigurative culture provides an opportunity to close the generation gap, since all generations are equally in search of a meaningful and stable life in an ever-changing and transient world.

As challenging as a prefigurative culture is, our current situation is far more complicated. The young generations now have access to a vast assortment of technologies that provide information (and misinformation) beyond anything known by elders, peers, or anyone else. Young people are increasingly linked to their computers, iPads, and smartphones. In some traditionalist societies, there are efforts to restrict use of technology among the young, but this effort is doomed to failure. Technology is ubiquitous, and no one can completely shut it out.

While methods will be found to harness technology in order to transmit knowledge, how will society be able to transmit its values? The technological universe provides a vast number of websites that promote violence, pornography, and moral relativism. Stories abound of young people who were lured by sexual predators, who committed suicide due to online bullying, or who were drawn into criminal or terroristic behavior.

Another by-product of the technological age is the incessant presence of cell phones, text messages, and emails. Professor Sherry Turkle of MIT has written an important book, *Reclaiming Conversation: The Power of Talk in a Digital Age.*[2] People have become so accustomed to communicating via technology, they have diminished their ability to communicate by talking face to face with others. People use their cell phones in social settings, even though they know this puts a damper on conversation. In 2010, a team at the University of Michigan led by psychologist Sara Konrath put together the findings of seventy-two studies that had been conducted over a thirty-year period. They found a 40 percent drop in empathy among college students, with most of the decline occurring after 2000. When people lose eye-to-eye contact with those with whom they converse, they also lessen the human interrelationship. Electronic communication, while it has its many advantages, also has the capacity to diminish our sense of empathy and genuine relationship with others.

Professor Turkle wisely calls for us to reclaim face-to-face conversation, to put away our cell phones while we speak with others, and to actually focus on the person with whom we are speaking. This is a step toward reclaiming our humanity, our sense of empathy and interrelatedness.

King Solomon advised long ago that discipline is a vital ingredient in education. Parents must give direction to their children; teachers must maintain order in their classes. This ought to be done not through corporal punishment but through strong and clear words. Children need to learn that they have responsibilities, that there are moral guidelines to which they must adhere. If children learn proper values and habits early in life, they will carry these qualities into their adulthood. They will develop self-discipline, which will enable them to achieve more and to be more confident and happier human beings. If we want our children and grandchildren to grow up into thoughtful, self-motivated, and empathetic human beings, our best gift to them is to guide them in a responsible and affirming way.

The world has changed, and continues to change, in dramatic ways, far beyond what King Solomon could have imagined. And yet, his basic advice is as sound today as it was thousands of years ago.

Understanding Ourselves ... and Others

The heart knows its own bitterness; and with its joy no stranger can intermeddle.

(PROVERBS 14:10)

The fast day of Yom Kippur is solemn and serious. One does not eat or drink on this day unless there is a serious medical emergency.

Jewish legal codes discuss the case of a person who is quite ill. If the doctor states that this person must not fast, then she may not fast. If the doctor states that the patient is not in fact seriously ill and that fasting would not endanger her health, then she should fast. But what if the doctor says that the patient is healthy enough to fast but the patient herself states that she is too sick to fast? The law is that in this case we listen to the patient, not to the doctor. Why? Because "the heart knows its own bitterness." A doctor only knows the patient's symptoms from an external vantage point. The patient alone knows the situation from the inside.

Although we sometimes delude ourselves as to our actual feelings, very often we understand our real selves better than anyone else does. Who can penetrate into our inner feelings? Who really grasps the depth of our sorrow or pain or the ecstasy of our joys and satisfactions? Only very few of the closest and most intimate of friends can really understand us.

The philosopher Martin Buber viewed humanity through the prism of our relationships. In his book *I and Thou*, he notes that many of our relationships are essentially utilitarian and functional.[1] We see the other as an "It." We are not interested in a deep relationship but simply want to use the other person. The other is a customer, or a provider of services, or an audience. By contrast, there are special relationships that are in the category of I-Thou, relationships where two people interact with mutual respect and understanding. In the I-It relationships, we are unable to penetrate to the other's true self; we are not even interested in this kind of relationship. Only in an I-Thou setting can we hope to understand and be understood by another person.

The Talmud (*Hagigah* 13a) teaches that the most esoteric knowledge can only be passed on to someone who has remarkable gifts of intellect and moral character. Among the qualities is that he must be a *sar hamishim*, a leader of fifty people. This does not refer to someone who gives assignments to these fifty individuals. Rather, it refers to a person who has the unique capacity to actually understand fifty people in the depths of who they are. Such knowledge cannot be gained through small talk and quick interactions. Rather, the *sar hamishim* has the capacity, patience, and wisdom to really come to know the inner feelings of these fifty people to the extent possible. How many of us can reach this level of interrelationships? It is quite a challenge to reach such a relationship with even one or a few people, let alone with fifty.

In my many years serving as a rabbi, I have known colleagues who genuinely give fully of themselves in order to understand the members of their communities. They gain the trust of congregants because people know the rabbi cares about them, listens to them, is vitally concerned for their well-being. But I have also known colleagues who spent little time trying to develop I-Thou relationships with their congregants. For such rabbis, congregants were simply a group of "Its." They paid their salary, listened to their sermons, and attended their classes. Such rabbis speak to—not with—their congregants. They speak, but seldom listen; and even when they listen, they don't listen carefully enough.

Although we know that very few special individuals will ever come near to understanding who we are and what our inner feelings are, we long to be discovered.

Role Models—Positive and Negative

He who oppresses the poor blasphemes his Maker; but he who is gracious unto the needy honors Him.

(PROVERBS 14:31)

Whoever stops his ears at the cry of the poor, he also shall cry himself but will not be answered.

(PROVERBS 21:13)

One who digs a pit shall fall into it; and he who rolls a stone, it shall return upon him.

(PROVERBS 26:27)

Remove not the ancient landmark; and enter not into the fields of orphans; for their Redeemer is strong; He will plead their cause against you.

(PROVERBS 23:10–11)

The sacrifice of the wicked is an abomination to the Lord; but the prayer of the upright is His delight.

(PROVERBS 15:8)

There are many devices in a man's heart; but it is the counsel of the Lord that shall stand.

(PROVERBS 19:21)

The Talmud (*Yoma* 86a) quotes the sage Abaye, who taught that the name of heaven should be made beloved by those who serve the Almighty:

> If someone studies Scripture and Mishnah and attends the disciples of the wise, is honest in business and speaks pleasantly to others, what do people say concerning this person? "Happy the father who taught him Torah, happy the teacher who taught him Torah. Woe unto those who have not studied Torah. This person has studied Torah and see how fine are his ways, how righteous his behavior." But the reverse is also true. If a religious person behaves crudely, dishonestly, and immorally, people are turned away from Torah and godliness. They say: "Woe unto him who studied Torah, woe unto his father who taught him Torah; woe unto his teacher who taught him Torah. This person studied Torah and look how corrupt are his deeds and how ugly his ways."

It is disheartening to learn of people who behave dishonestly, who oppress the poor, who act violently. It is all the more disheartening when these people have the veneer of being religious. The charge of religious hypocrisy undermines religion. If so-called religious people act in unseemly ways, then the value of religion itself is called into question.

King Solomon notes that when wicked people offer sacrifices and prayers to God, these are abominations. How dare they stand before God with unclean hands? How dare they feign piety when their immoral behavior belies the teachings of Torah?

It is said of the great sixteenth-century kabbalist Rabbi Yitzhak Luria that he would not recite his afternoon prayers until after he paid his day laborers for their work. He reasoned: How can I stand before God and pray when I am guilty of not having paid my workers on time? A religious person needs to have the conscience of Rabbi Luria.

Unfortunately, there is no shortage of religious people—including clergy—who cause public desecration of the name of God. They may mouth the right words, but their deeds do not conform to the ideals that they claim to espouse. I suppose that many—if not all—of us have had a negative experience with a "religious hypocrite." They appear so self-righteous and so pious; and yet they have no qualms about cheating, lying, or engaging in criminal behavior.

It is even more irksome when we see that these hypocrites actually succeed in maintaining their communal status. In his essay about the eighteenth-century French novelist and dramatist Pierre de Marivaux, Dr. Rene Girard points out how Marivaux's heroes are guilty of hypocrisy and bad faith—and yet are deemed to be popular and successful by their peers. He quotes Marivaux:

> But oh! How I hate, how I detest those vain and deceitful people whose tricks are so clever, whose impostures are so well devised that almost everybody sides with them and one does not know how to cast upon them the opprobrium they deserve.[1]

Hypocrites may be able to fool others. They may even be able to fool themselves. But they cannot fool Almighty God. "There are many devices in a man's heart; but it is the counsel of the Lord that shall stand" (Proverbs 19:21).

Developing the "Self"

He who is slow to anger is better than the mighty; and he
who rules his spirit than one who takes a city.

(PROVERBS 16:32)

In my book *Losing the Rat Race, Winning at Life*, I wrote:

> During the course of a lifetime, a person may wear many
> masks. In order to curry favor with others, one adopts
> their attitudes, opinions, styles and behavior patterns.
> Above all, one wants to belong, to play an acceptable role.
> At the same time, one also has a separate individual iden-
> tity within, the hard kernel of one's own being. When one
> loses sight of his separateness from the masks he wears,
> he becomes the masks; i.e., a superficial, artificial human
> being. A person may go through life without examining
> carefully who he really is. One simply becomes an assort-
> ment of ever-changing masks, living life on the surface.[1]

Rabbinic tradition offers an interpretation of Genesis 12:1, where
God commands Abram to leave his land, his birthplace, his father's
house, to go to a new land to which God will direct him. The
Hebrew text begins, *Lekh lekha*, which is normally translated to
mean "get thee out" or "get yourself going." Yet, the text can also
be read more literally as "go to yourself," that is, to your own self.
In order to start off on his new road of life, Abram was told that he
first had to go into himself, find out who he was at his core.

   Our "self" cannot realistically be separated from the influences of
others, such as parents, relatives, friends, or teachers. It is the task
of the "self" to understand, evaluate, accept, or reject the external
influences on our life.

It is not easy to separate ourselves from our masks. Our self-definition is vastly influenced by the opinions of others. Much human misery comes as a result of people betraying themselves by adopting artificial personae. They present themselves as intellectuals, business tycoons, or gregarious show-offs. Yet, deep down they know themselves to be only moderately intelligent and creative, or they detest the world of business competition, or they know that they prefer quiet conversation in small groups rather than noisy talk in big crowds.

People are happiest when they respect themselves, when they feel they have taken responsibility for their lives and have done well. Ralph Waldo Emerson wrote that "there is a time in every man's education when he arrives at the conviction that envy is ignorance; that imitation is suicide; that he must take himself for better and for worse as his portion."[2]

If we wish to live life on its deepest level, we must be able to stand on our own, without allowing the attitudes and values of others to supplant personal attitudes and values. In one way or another, everyone wears masks; yet the wise person knows not to confuse the self with the masks. A wise person "rules his spirit," has control over his inner life, and has the strength to stand alone.

When a person acts in an artificial manner in order to pose as an authentic human being, he is clearly a play actor rather than a real human being. When an artist becomes self-conscious of being an artist, he loses the quality of being a genuine artist. The same is true of a religious personality. An artist, a poet, a religious person is always striving to express some deep feelings or ideas for which his expressions are inadequate. He tries again and again, and always—at least to himself—fails. Once he thinks he has succeeded—if only for an instant—in that instant he is no longer an artist, a poet, a religious personality. Vanity has obscured his humility. But it is humility and the sense of inadequacy that serve as the foundation of spiritual greatness.

No two human beings are exactly alike. It is precisely our individualistic worldviews that enable each of us to make a distinctive contribution to society. Our sense of meaning in life is directly correlated with our freedom to participate creatively in the human adventure.

Rabbinic commentators wonder why, when God commands Abram to go "unto the land that I will show you," God did not specify the destination to which He was sending Abram. The general consensus is that God was testing Abram's faith: would he leave his land and birthplace and father's home to go to some vague destination?

I interpret this command to Abram in a broader sense, as applying to every human being. We are each commanded to pick ourselves up and head for an unspecified destination; it is unspecified because each of us has a different place to reach. Each of us needs to find that inner wholeness that comes with trying to reach the goals that the Almighty had in mind for us. If we are true to our inner light, if we strive to maximize our talents and energies, then we will find ourselves moving in the direction of that mysterious land that "I will show you."

Grandparents and Grandchildren

Children's children are the crown of old men; and the
glory of children are their fathers.

(PROVERBS 17:6)

In one of his lectures, Rabbi Joseph B. Soloveitchik mused on the
relationship between grandparents and grandchildren: "A grandfather stands before his newly born grandchild filled with paradoxical
thoughts. Feelings of renewal merge with fading memories of the
past."[1]

A grandparent gazes at grandchildren with a sense of wonder.
Fifty, sixty, and more years separate them. The grandparent is part
of the old generation, while the grandchildren are part of a new
world with new challenges and opportunities. Yes, the grandparent
feels a sense of family continuity—but also a sense of anxiety. Will
we—of different generations—feel a sense of harmony, a common
history and destiny? Will we be able to talk to each other heart to
heart? Or will alienation set in? Will the grandchildren have different
life agendas than we have?

The larger question is, how can we hold our community and culture together from generation to generation? How do we avoid the
ubiquitous problem of the generation gap? The Mishnah (*Eduyot*
2:9) cites the opinion of Rabbi Akiva, who stated that parents transmit six characteristics to their children, including physical appearance, strength, wealth, wisdom, and longevity. The sixth quality is
mispar ha-dorot lefanav, "the number of generations before them."
But what exactly does this mean?

Children are not born into a historical vacuum. They are heirs to
the generations of their family going back through the centuries and
millennia. In the case of Jewish children (and grandchildren), they

118

not only are heirs to their particular family's traditions, but inherit all the earlier generations of the Jewish people going back to the time of Abraham and Sarah.

The challenge to the older generations is to transmit to the new generations a feeling of connectedness with the past. We introduce our children and grandchildren to "the number of generations before them" so that they come to see the biblical characters of thousands of years ago as part of their own group of close friends. We teach them that *we* were slaves in Egypt; that *we* were redeemed; that *we* built the Temples in Jerusalem; that *we* went into exile. Rashi and Rambam are *our* teachers. Our earlier generations continue to live in our memories and are a presence in our lives. We want our children and grandchildren to understand that they are engaged in a lifelong dialogue among all the generations of their family and of their people. What a wonderful gift to give children!

In a traditional religious setting, there need not be a generation gap where alienation sets in between the generations. In some unique, mysterious way, the different generations see themselves as contemporaries. We share a spiritual outlook, a set of ideals, a style of living according to the Torah. We cherish the gift of "the number of generations before us."

The Generation of the Lie

He who justifies the wicked and he who condemns the
righteous, even they both are an abomination to the Lord.

(PROVERBS 17:15)

Death and life are in the power of the tongue; and they
who indulge it shall eat the fruit thereof.

(PROVERBS 18:21)

The United States suffered a horrible and horrifying terrorist attack
on September 11, 2001. Arab terrorists flew airplanes into the Twin
Towers, killing thousands of people. Two other airplanes were
hijacked, leading to the murder of all the passengers.

Moral clarity prevailed in many circles. The terrorists were murderers, hateful and misguided individuals who believed that they
would be rewarded in heaven if they murdered Americans. They
were willing to sacrifice their own lives for the sake of inflicting
damage on the United States. But, there were those who justified
the wicked and who condemned the righteous. They described the
murderers as "martyrs." They rejoiced that America, the great devil,
had suffered a serious blow.

The same pattern often is evident when acts of terror are committed against Israel. The murderers are described as "militants" or
as "martyrs." The Israeli victims are blamed for their own deaths,
and the murderers are honored by the societies from which they
emerged. The United Nations routinely condemns Israel for defend-
ing itself against terrorism and routinely ignores the heinous acts of
murder committed against Israel.

We should not be surprised by the massive hypocrisy that justifies the wicked and condemns the righteous. This has been going on for many centuries. Not only does Solomon note this phenomenon in Proverbs, his father David screamed out against it in his Psalms. Psalm 12 has been described by Martin Buber as a prophecy "against the generation of the lie." The Psalmist cries out, "Help, O Lord, for the pious cease to be.... They speak falsehood each with his neighbor, with flattering lip, with a double heart they speak" (Psalm 12:2–3). The generation is led by oppressors who say "our tongue will make us mighty" (v. 5), who arrogantly crush the downtrodden. They act sinfully but are confident that their smooth-talking propaganda will keep them immune from retribution.

Buber comments:

> They speak with a double heart, literally "with heart and heart."... The duplicity is not just between heart and mouth, but actually between heart and heart. In order that the lie may bear the stamp of truth, the liars as it were manufacture a special heart, an apparatus which functions with the greatest appearance of naturalness, from which lies well up to the "smooth lips" like spontaneous utterances of experience and insight.[1]

The Psalmist is condemning not merely his "generation of the lie," but future generations that also will be characterized by lying, bullying, oppressing; that will be led by smooth-talking and corrupt demagogues. But the Psalmist turns prophet and proclaims that God will arise and protect the victims of the liars. Truth will prevail. "It is You, O Lord, who will guard the poor, You will protect us forever from this generation" (Psalm 12:8).

Although the Psalmist is confident that God will set things right, meanwhile the ugly fact remains: "But the wicked will strut around when vileness is exalted among humankind" (Psalm 12:9). Although God will ultimately redeem the world from the "generation of the lie," this will not happen right away. As long as people submit to the rule of the wicked, the wicked will stay in power. If the wicked are not resisted, they will continue to strut around and feel invincible.

The Nazis understood the power of propaganda. If you tell a big lie often enough and loud enough, people begin to believe it. Even if they do not fully believe it, they will lose the spiritual courage to resist the liars. They either will remain passive or will actively conspire with the wicked. The "generation of the lie" continues to flourish in our day, when tyrannies are viewed favorably and democracies are judged negatively. Every vote that justifies wickedness is an act of complicity with the wicked. Every abstention that refrains from condemning wickedness is also an act of complicity with the wicked.

Albert Einstein described the moral decay that he felt was setting into society:

> One misses the elementary reaction against injustice and for justice—that reaction which in the long run represents man's only protection against a relapse into barbarism. I am firmly convinced that the passionate will for justice and truth has done more to improve man's condition than calculating political shrewdness which in the long run only breeds general distrust. Who can doubt that Moses was a better leader of humanity than Machiavelli?[2]

The Dignity of Growing Old

*The glory of young men is their strength; and the beauty
of old men is the hoary head.*

(Proverbs 20:29)

While modern Western society places high value on youthfulness, traditional societies tended to venerate the elders. Men and women with gray hair were honored for having gained life wisdom through their many years of experience. The dignity of old age was something to which younger people aspired.

Dr. Atul Gawande has noted the phenomenon that demographers call "age heaping." Apparently, people have always tended to lie about their ages. Demographers have devised complex quantitative tools in order to correct the lying that invariably takes place when people fill out census forms. They have found that in the United States and Europe, the direction of our lies took a change during the eighteenth century. "Whereas today people often understate their age to census takers, studies of past censuses have revealed that they used to overstate it."[1] People *wanted* to be considered older; old age was something desirable.

That things have changed dramatically is obvious to anyone living in the Western world. The emphasis now is on youthfulness. People spend many billions of dollars on cosmetics and plastic surgery in order to look younger. They dye their hair, hide their wrinkles, act and dress as though they were much younger. Being old is often associated with being unproductive, incapacitated, or simply unable to keep up with the pace of the modern world.

At a time when life expectancy is rising in modern societies, more people are growing old. Instead of learning to accept and value this phenomenon, many elders seek ways of denying their advancing years. They pretend to be younger, but they rarely fool anyone except themselves—and usually, not even themselves!

When I turned seventy, I wrote a short essay musing about growing old. I posted it on the website of the Institute for Jewish Ideas and Ideals (jewishideas.org). Following is the text of that essay.

> Rabbi Elazar ben Azaryah said: Here I am as a man of seventy years old, yet I was not privileged to know the source of the commandment to recite the story of the Exodus from Egypt at night, until Ben Zoma interpreted the verse. The Torah states (Deuteronomy 16:3), "So that you will remember the day you went out from the land of Egypt *all* the days of your life." If the verse had stated "the days of your life," I would understand the commandment to refer to days. Since it adds the word "all," this comes to include nights. The sages have interpreted the verse as follows: The days of your life refers to this world; *all* the days of your life comes to include the days of the Messiah. (*Mishnah Berakhot* 1:5)

The above Talmudic passage, well known due to its inclusion in the text of the Passover Haggadah, relates to Rabbi Elazar ben Azaryah. The sages of Yavneh, during the period following the destruction of the Second Temple in Jerusalem, wanted to appoint Rabbi Elazar ben Azaryah as head of the Academy. He was a brilliant scholar, respected and beloved by his colleagues. But he had one shortcoming: he was too young! It was considered inappropriate to have such a young man as head of the venerable Rabbinic sages of Yavneh.

The Talmud relates that a miracle happened. The young Rabbi Elazar ben Azaryah woke up one morning and found that his hair and his beard had turned gray! He now looked like an elder. When his colleagues viewed his new appearance, they then felt comfortable asking him to become head of the Academy of Yavneh.

So Rabbi Elazar ben Azaryah had the best of both worlds: he was chronologically a young man, full of the strength and energy of youth; but he was also (at least in appearance) an old man, filled with the experience and sagacity of age.

What a great combination! What a wonderful blessing to be young and old at the same time!

Rabbi Elazar ben Azaryah, once he was "as a man of seventy years old," realized something very important, something he had learned from Ben Zoma. One is obligated to recite the story of the Exodus from Egypt at night. This lesson, I believe, goes beyond the technical issue of when to recite the Haggadah. It reflects a religious worldview.

Night symbolizes the time of darkness, the crises and sad moments of life. At night, things seem bleak, even frightening. Rabbi Elazar ben Azaryah came to understand that even at the "nights" of life, we must recite the story of redemption. We must look forward to the coming dawn. We must see beyond the darkness and envision the brightness and glory yet to come.

The secret of being young and old simultaneously is maintaining hope, looking ahead, overcoming gloom and failure by focusing on the brightness on the horizon.

A wit once said: You don't stop laughing when you get old; you get old when you stop laughing. This can be rephrased: You don't stop dreaming and growing when you get old; you get old when you stop dreaming and growing.

It is a great blessing to reach age seventy. One can look back on a long span of life's joys and achievements. But one, inevitably, also looks back on a long span of life's sad times and personal failings.

I thank the Almighty for having brought me to this special stage of my life. I don't have adequate words to express my joy and gratitude to my wife, Gilda, to our children and grandchildren, to our relatives and friends who have made life so worthwhile and so satisfying. I thank all those who have been steadfast and loyal in their friendship over these many years. I am grateful for the special people and the special moments of my life. My cup overflows.

But one cannot reach age seventy without having experienced sadness and loss. I remember with profound love my late parents, grandparents, uncles, and aunts; my parents-in-law and so many relatives and friends who have passed on to their eternal reward. I sometimes quip that I have more friends in the next world than I do in this world; although this is just a quip, it has a lot of truth in it. So many loved ones and real friends have died, but their memories continue to inspire.

One of the common features of aging is a sense of contraction. One's physical strength isn't what it used to be. One's circle of relatives and friends changes—and often contracts—as the mysteries of life and death play out. One's professional life changes—and often contracts—as one grows older.

So I find great satisfaction in thinking about Rabbi Elazar ben Azaryah's ability to be young and old at the same time. I find great meaning in his lesson to overcome darkness by envisioning the coming redemption.

In a sense, I feel that I have a reverse situation to that of Rabbi Elazar ben Azaryah. I *am* a man of seventy years old, and yet I thank the Almighty that I have the enthusiasm, optimism, and energy of someone much younger in years. Instead of letting life contract, I have been very fortunate to keep expanding the scope of life, through our growing family, through my work for the Institute for Jewish Ideas and Ideals, and through my ongoing writing, teaching, and lecturing. I pray that the Almighty will bless me with additional years of learning, growing, and sharing.

The messianic era has not yet arrived. There is much work to do, many challenges ahead. I am grateful for the many wonderful yesterdays of life. I pray to be worthy of many wonderful tomorrows, together with Gilda and our family, our loved ones, and our true and trusted friends.

When People Disappoint You

Confidence in an unfaithful man in time of trouble is like
a broken tooth and a foot out of joint.

(PROVERBS 25:19)

One of the most painful experiences in life is to be betrayed by
someone you had trusted—a loved one, a close friend, a teacher,
a clergyperson. You had been confident of that person's goodwill
toward you. You believed in that person's loyalty, honesty, and
moral character. But that special person has now caused you grief.

When confronting an overt enemy, you at least know the enemy
is out to hurt or destroy you. You brace yourself for attacks and
vilifications. You do not expect kindness and understanding from a
hostile party.

But when a trusted person turns on you, it hurts so much more.
It is not just that you face a new antagonist; it is that your confidence in the goodness of humanity is undermined. If this person
turned on you, can you ever trust anyone? We identify with King
David, who cried out when he was betrayed, "Even my ally in
whom I trusted, who shared my bread, has been exceedingly false to
me" (Psalm 41:10).

Moses himself faced a similar dilemma. His most loyal allies were
members of his own family and his own tribe, the tribe of Levi. And
yet, Korah led a rebellion against Moses. As Rabbi Adin Steinsaltz
has well noted:

> The disputes until now have always been with outsiders,
> and Moses can basically relate to them with equanimity.
> Korah, however, is not an outsider; he is Moses' cousin,
> a relative. When such a dispute comes from within, it is
> much more painful.[1]

Even if we intellectually know that people are fickle and that relationships can come apart, we do not think betrayals will happen to us. When they do, we feel as though we have been punched hard in the stomach; we gasp for breath. How will we recover from this shocking blow?

We learn all too often about trusted officials who have committed crimes; about teachers and clergy who have been guilty of egregious conduct; about "honorable" businesspeople who have cheated and robbed their clients and associates. Recent scandals in the rabbinic world have caused untold distress to so many people who had looked up to and trusted their rabbis.

In his powerful article "When Leaders Fail," Rabbi Yitzchak Breitowitz describes the grievous consequences of religious leadership that falls short of the Torah ideals. Rabbi Breitowitz notes the destructive nature of pride and overconfidence and the dangers of charisma and the personality cult. When religious leaders become smug, they come to feel immune to communal sanction. They lose sight of proper moral boundaries, thinking that they are not accountable to anyone. They seek power and prestige; they seek to control; they do not function as humble servants of God or as loyal servants of the public. Rabbi Breitowitz points out:

> Erudition, scholarship and personal magnetism are no guarantee of spirituality and inner goodness.... If one is imbued with compassion, kindness and humility, then Torah study will make him more so. If one is competitive, arrogant and self-aggrandizing, Torah scholarship will simply create another battlefield in which those qualities can be expressed.... All of this suggests that communities must pay much closer attention to the moral qualities and personality traits of the leaders and role models that they choose. That certain flashy qualities might be overvalued in the selection process while other qualities—gentleness, modesty—are undervalued or even disparaged will only hurt the community in the long run.[2]

How do we heal from the betrayal of loved ones, friends, leaders, and others whom we had implicitly trusted?

In many ways, the loss of trust in a person who has betrayed us is akin to dealing with the death of a loved one. There is shock, grief, disbelief that such a tragedy has actually occurred. The work of mourning entails coming to grips with reality, gradually reaching acceptance of the new loss. During this painful process, we may feel guilt: could I have done something differently; was the betrayal a result of my own errors in judgment? We may feel angry: How could he behave so callously after all that I've done for him? How could she turn on me after I stood by her when she was in distress? We may feel foolish: Why didn't I see her faults much sooner? Why was I so blind to his essential untrustworthiness?

While the mourning process varies from person to person, most are able to absorb the loss and go on with life in a positive way. Likewise, when we suffer the betrayal of a trusted person, we eventually need to come to accept the new reality and go on with our lives in a productive way.

Many years ago, a member of our congregation taught me an important lesson. Whenever he faced suffering and loss, he would say, "Turn the page." Life is a book. If we stay stuck in one place or if we keep rereading the past chapters, we are not living properly. "Turn the page"—go on to the next stage of life, and do not dwell on the past. The greatest way to frustrate our betrayers is to "turn the page," to keep moving on with our lives, happily and strongly.

Standing Up to Bullies

Answer not a fool according to his folly, lest you also be like him. Answer a fool according to his folly, lest he be wise in his own eyes.

(PROVERBS 26:4–5)

When confronted by a foolish person who makes foolish remarks, Solomon advises to avoid getting into a discussion or argument. This refers to general foolishness that has no ramifications. But if the fool makes false claims or espouses dangerous views, the fool must be refuted. Staying silent in the face of egregious lies is morally repugnant. Silence signifies either consent or cowardice.

When liars and bullies spew their nonsense, it takes courage to stand up against them. Demagogues intimidate the masses. Many follow along; many stay silent. Yet, if they are not resisted, they become "wise in their own eyes." An episode in the Torah sheds light on this phenomenon.

When the Israelites pressed Aaron to make them an idol of gold, the Torah informs us, "And all the people broke off the golden rings that were in their ears and brought them to Aaron" (Exodus 32:3). It seems that "all the people" participated in idolatrous behavior.

Yet, when it came to contributing to the building of the *Mishkan*, the sanctuary of God, the Torah states that donations were to be given only by those with generous hearts, "of every person whose heart was willing" (Exodus 25:2). The donations came not from "all the people" but from a smaller group of willing donors.

Professor Yeshaya Leibowitz, in his book *Accepting the Yoke of Heaven*, offers his interpretation as to why these events differed.[1] Simply stated, it is much easier to get drawn into doing evil than into doing something righteous. Once the Israelites went into a frenzy to make an idol, "all the people" were swept up in the excitement; all of them contributed quickly and generously. But when it came to building the *Mishkan*, some were reluctant to part with their valuables. There are mental obstacles to contributing to a worthy cause. Donors need to battle with internal resistance. They need to let their generosity overcome their possessiveness.

Professor Leibowitz's observation is bolstered by the Midrash. At the time of the golden calf, the Israelites had two main leaders in the absence of Moses: Aaron and Hur. The Midrash posits that Hur resisted the idolatrous masses, and they murdered him! Seeing this, Aaron decided it was safer to go along with the crowd rather than to stand up against them. Hur died a martyr's death. Aaron, who went along with the sinning crowd, survived and even went on to serve as High Priest (*Exodus Rabbah* 41:7).

Yet, I wonder if "all the people" who contributed their gold earrings really were ideologically convinced to engage in idolatry. I suspect that a rather small group made the decision and usurped the leadership. When no one (other than Hur) stood up against them, they became increasingly arrogant. They murdered Hur to set an example: resistance doesn't pay. They cowed the masses of Israelites, who handed in their gold earrings because they were too afraid to resist or because they were too apathetic to fight the in-group. Their participation wasn't enthusiastic and ideologically motivated; it was more like a passive going along with the tide.

It is easier to go along with evil than to stand up defiantly against evil.

It is easier to join with bullies or to look the other way, rather than to confront them.

A recent study has reported that being severely bullied is quite common for many students. Forty-one percent of middle school and high school students in the United States report that they were bullied at least once during their current school term. About 11 percent of boys report that they are bullied once a week or more. Of the boys who report being bullied, nearly 18 percent are hit, slapped, or pushed once a week or more.[2]

The easier it is for bullies to cow their victims, the easier it is for them to continue their bullying. If the victims are too weak or too afraid to resist, the bullies are emboldened to increase their arrogance and their violence.

But it's not just the inability of victims to resist; it's the inability or unwillingness of all the witnesses to come to the aid of the victims. The masses, by their passivity, allow the bullies to flourish and to create an environment of fear. Some attempt to befriend the bullies, to protect themselves from being bullied. Others feel too weak to confront the bullies, so they look the other way. Those who stand up to the bullies run the risk of being beaten up and humiliated in the eyes of others.

It is easier to go along with the tide than to stand up in righteous opposition. It is easier to donate gold earrings for a golden calf than to incur the wrath of the wicked clique that is leading the idolatrous movement.

From the days of the golden calf to our own times, bullies have attempted to assert their leadership by means of violence and instilling fear. They have depended on the weakness of the victims to resist. Even more, they have depended on the silent majority that lacks the courage to stand tall.

Bullying takes many forms in our society. Sometimes it is overtly violent. Sometimes it is the surreptitious usurpation of power by undermining all opposition. Sometimes it shows itself in tyrants and dictators, and sometimes it shows itself in power-hungry individuals in all walks of life. The common denominator is that bullies prevail by crushing or intimidating opposition.

There are many people today, in all walks of life, who call on us to donate our "gold earrings" to create all sorts of "golden calves." Are we donating, or are we rallying our courage and our morality so that we can resist?

Egomaniacs and Their Masks

Let another man praise you, and not your own mouth; a stranger, and not your own lips.

(PROVERBS 27:2)

Among the most annoying people are those who speak in praise of themselves. They brag, they boast about their accomplishments, they remind us that their children are brilliant. They constantly speak of their illustrious ancestors. They frequently mention the important people they know or the prestigious schools they attended. They try ever so hard to impress us. In the process, though, we are repelled. We feel sorry for these pathetic figures whose self-images are so weak that they feel the need to constantly prove how great they are.

When self-absorbed people with weak egos brag about themselves, we can stop listening to them. A problem arises, though, when these people try to assert their importance by abusing others. An article by Professor Christine Porath discusses key research on the nature of effective leadership. She notes how incivility in the workplace leads to demoralization and a decline in quality of productivity. A survey of forty-five hundred doctors, nurses, and other hospital personnel found that 71 percent tied medical errors to abusive, condescending, or insulting conduct by those in authority; 27 percent tied such behavior to patient deaths![1]

Various studies have demonstrated a sharp decline in efficiency and effectiveness when employees are treated with incivility. They have shown that "the number one characteristic associated with an executive's failure is an insensitive, abrasive or bullying style."[2] Such executives may think that rudeness and crude shows of power are signs of strength; in fact, these are the very qualities that undermine the success of those executives. They have not understood that a leader needs to be strong but also gentle and sensitive to the needs and feelings of others.

What is true in hospitals and industry is even truer in religious institutions. When the shepherds, whether rabbinic or lay, serve the community with selflessness, idealism, and sensitivity, the result is a harmonious community where everyone feels valued and respected. When the shepherds, whether rabbinic or lay, behave in a callous and smug manner, the community becomes demoralized. When the community feels that the shepherds are more interested in their own power than in the needs of the people, the community begins to unravel. Demoralized people stray away, lose confidence, stop attending, and stop contributing. Without genuinely devoted shepherds, "the flock of the Lord" loses direction.

The braggarts of the world are flawed human beings. At root, they live with fear and insecurity. They wear a mask of confidence, but beneath the mask there is a frightened ego.

In describing the impact of a mask on its wearer, Elias Canetti notes:

> As long as he wears it he is two things, himself and the mask.... Because it can be torn away, its wearer is bound to fear for it. He must take care that he does not lose it; it must never be dropped and must never open. He feels every kind of anxiety about what may happen to it.... He must manipulate it, remaining his everyday self, and, at the same time, must change into it as a performer. While he wears the mask he is thus two people and must remain two during the whole of his performance.[3]

At some point, the masks of the braggarts and the power hungry will come off. Either they will be torn off, or wise people will simply see right through them. The self-promoting and self-serving boors will learn that their masks fool no one ... not even themselves.

A Woman of Valor

Whoso finds a wife finds a great good, and obtains favor of the Lord.

(Proverbs 18:22)

A woman of valor who can find? For her price is far above rubies.

(Proverbs 31:10)

Grace is deceitful, and beauty is vain; but a woman who fears the Lord, she shall be praised. Give her of the fruit of her hands; and let her works praise her in the gates.

(Proverbs 31:30–31)

My mother, Rachel Romey Angel, was born in 1914 in Seattle, Washington, the second of seven children born to Marco and Sultana Romey—both immigrants from Turkey. Although my grandparents were born and raised in Turkey, their first language was Judeo-Spanish, the language of the Sephardic Jews scattered throughout the former Ottoman Empire. My mother did not learn to speak English until she attended kindergarten in public school.

The Sephardic immigrants of Seattle came to America with little money and little formal education but with a tremendous desire to make a new and better life for themselves and their families. The first-generation immigrants worked at various trades; their children went on to own stores and other businesses; their grandchildren were nearly all university-educated professionals and businesspeople.

My mother was "only a girl." In those days and in that society, it was assumed that girls would marry at an early age and have families of their own. Girls did not need much education, only basic domestic skills such as cooking and sewing. In the milieu of my mother's childhood, it was highly unusual for a woman to attend university or to hold a serious job outside the home.

My mother was a brilliant student, but when she turned sixteen—the legal age until which one was required to attend school—my grandfather told her she had to quit school and get a job to help support the family. Her older sister had done that and was working in a candy factory, and my grandfather wanted my mother to do likewise. My mother told her teachers at Garfield High School that she was going to be leaving school to go to work. One of the teachers was so distressed by this news that she spoke with my grandfather, urging him to let my mother graduate from high school. She told him that his daughter was a wonderful student with an excellent mind; if given the opportunity, she could attend university and do great things with her life. My grandfather replied, "She's only a girl; she doesn't need more education. She has to go to work and earn money."

Thus ended my mother's academic career. She never graduated from high school. She worked in the candy factory for a few years, got married at age twenty-one, and went on to have four children and eventually twelve grandchildren. She was a voracious reader, a deep thinker, and a keen observer of human nature. Neither her husband nor their close group of friends had a college graduate among them, so my mother was sort of a closet intellectual. She functioned happily and successfully in her world, but she kept her intellectual, philosophical side pretty much to herself. If she had been born two generations later, she would have been a university graduate, probably a PhD, and she would have had opportunities in academia, public life, or business that were totally out of reach for her in her time and place.

Was my mother a success? Was she happy? Did she fulfill her mission in life? The answer to these questions depends on how we evaluate success, happiness, and fulfillment in life. If we deem someone successful, happy, and fulfilled if she earned a good income, lived a prosperous life, earned an academic degree, and held responsible positions in professional life, then my mother did not meet these requirements.

But my mother was a remarkable woman. She was a loyal daughter, devoted wife, loving mother and grandmother, gracious hostess, excellent friend. She was a profound thinker, an avid reader, a talented knitter. She enjoyed the simple pleasures of life. She was good and kind, thoughtful, and highly principled. If measured by standards of quality rather than quantity, my mother was eminently successful, happy, and fulfilled in life.

When King Solomon praises the "woman of valor," he refers to the virtues of being a good wife and mother, a hard worker on behalf of her family, a generous soul who is charitable and kind. The Hebrew word for valor, *hayyil*, has the connotation of strength and courage. The "ideal" woman is identified not as being passive and obedient, but rather as having a strong character focused on her life's values and goals.

When reading the last passages of Proverbs today, we are struck by how much society has changed in recent generations. Women today have far more opportunities in education, professions, public life, and business than had been true for women in many societies of the past. But this success has also come with trade-offs. In pursuing careers, women may defer or forgo the joys of a solid marriage, child rearing, and being full-time mothers. Are the modern "liberated" women more successful, happier, and more fulfilled than the women of my mother's pattern of life? In some ways, yes; in other ways, probably not.

I remember reading somewhere that in our modern society a woman is considered creative if she produces a piece of sculpture or operates her own business. But if a woman is "merely" a mother who creates children, shapes their lives, and sees to it that they can lead happy and good lives, she is labeled somewhat pejoratively as "only being a housewife." A full-time wife and mother is deemed to be on a lower level than women who devote their energies to professional or business life.

If my mother had been given more opportunities to develop her intellect and talents, she would have had a significant impact on many people beyond her immediate circle of family and friends. She would have been gratified to learn more and teach more and to play a greater role in the larger society. She would have been very happy to have had many of the opportunities that were available to her own daughter, daughters-in-law, and granddaughters.

But despite that, her own life evaluated in its own context was a remarkably happy, meaningful, and successful adventure. She was grateful for what she had and what she was able to achieve. She was beautiful and graceful; she feared God; she loved and was loved; she raised and inspired her children; she left an indelible impact on her grandchildren. "She shall be praised" (Proverbs 31:30).

PART THREE

The Quest for Relationship with God

The Song of Songs/ Shir ha-Shirim

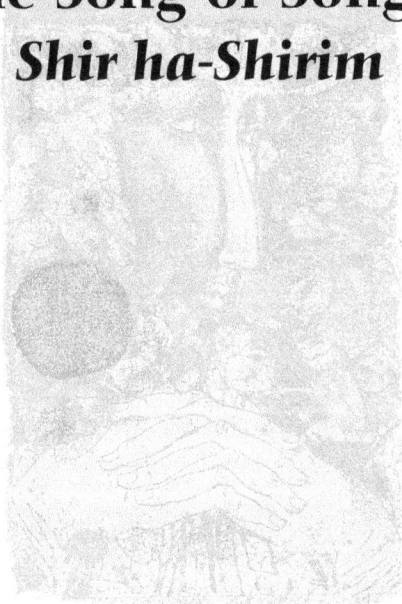

Finding Our Own Song

The Song of Songs, which is Solomon's.

(SONG OF SONGS 1:1)

Rabbinic tradition understands the Song of Songs as a profound song describing the love between God and Israel. It is also interpreted as a song expressing the yearnings of a person who is seeking a loving relationship with God. It is not merely Solomon's song but his loftiest song, the song above all other of his songs, the song that can inspire those who ponder its words.

The ultimate religious quest is put into the context of song. Each person has a distinctive song, a unique contribution to make to this world; this contribution is embodied in the person's philosophy, talents, and sensitivities. Symbolically, a person's unique contribution can be described as a song—a special personal melody that imbues life with meaning and purpose.

As composers of our own life song, we need to be faithful to our internal music. It is all too easy to suppress our voice in order to blend into the noise of the crowd. It is all too easy to fall under the sway of an authoritarian guru who quashes our own song and makes us sing his. It is also easy to fall into the trap of believing that we do not have a spiritual song to sing, that we are merely physical beings without a soul.

The great medieval philosopher Moses Maimonides offered keen insight on how an individual begins a relationship with the Almighty. In his *Mishneh Torah*, he teaches:

> When a person contemplates His great and wondrous works and creatures and from them obtains a glimpse of His wisdom which is incomparable and infinite, he will

straightaway love Him, praise Him, glorify Him, and long with an exceeding longing to know His great name ... and when he ponders these matters, he will recoil frightened and realize that he is a small creature, lowly and obscure, endowed with slight and slender intelligence, standing in the presence of Him who is perfect in knowledge. (Foundations of the Torah 2:2)

Love of God entails a transcendence of the self. We look at the star-filled sky, or at a glorious sunrise, or at a magnificent mountain or ocean, or into the eyes of a lion or tiger. We are alone in our thoughts. We let our mind drift as we sense the wonder of what we are seeing. How did these things come into being? What power keeps them in existence? As we contemplate these things, we feel a sudden epiphany. We sense that we are in the presence of God, and we long to feel part of God's cosmic wisdom. This is the seed of the love of God, the impulse toward a grand and transcendent unity. That feeling of love leads to the feeling of reverence: we are overpowered by the incomprehensible confrontation with the Eternal and the Infinite.

Interestingly, Maimonides describes the love and reverence of God as deriving from a personal experience with God's creations. At root, it is a quiet and private experience. It is a turning within the individual's soul. It is the cosmic music that fills one's being.

Surely we might feel love of God in the context of a large religious gathering, in the words of an eloquent preacher, or in the pious deeds of good people. But Maimonides underscores the essential and personal confrontation with the God of the universe, the God of nature. When we are silent and alone, when we don't hear any other voices—that is the time when we might hear the voice of God. That is the time when we might begin to compose our own spiritual song.

Deveikut–Clinging to God

Let him kiss me with the kisses of his mouth, for your love is better than wine.

(SONG OF SONGS 1:2)

The Midrash (*Song of Songs Rabbah* 1:2) interprets this verse as referring to the desire to cling to God—*deveikut*. Rabbi Moshe Almosnino (sixteenth century, Salonika) states that the "kisses"— that is, direct experiences with God—are more joyful and more intoxicating than wine.[1]

The Torah teaches, "You shall fear the Lord your God; Him shall you serve, and to Him shall you cleave, and by His name shall you swear" (Deuteronomy 10:20). The instruction to "cling" or to "cleave" to God is also found in Deuteronomy 13:5 and 30:20. The Talmud asks, how is it possible for a mortal human being to cling to the eternal and infinite God? One answer is that we cannot cling directly to God, but we can attach ourselves to godly people (Talmud, *Ketubot* 111b). Another answer is that we should imitate the positive qualities ascribed to God: just as God is compassionate, so we should be compassionate; just as God is merciful, so we should be merciful (Talmud, *Sotah* 14a).

In kabbalistic literature, the concept of *deveikut*—clinging to God—has the connotation of experiencing communion with God. This is achieved at times of heightened prayer and meditation, when one's mind is totally focused on the Almighty. In Jewish legal literature, *deveikut* is understood in a similar manner. Rabbi Joseph Karo in his *Shulhan Arukh*—the classic code of Jewish law—instructs the one who prays to

> imagine that the Divine Presence is with him. He should remove all thoughts that trouble him, and his thought and

143

concentration are pure in his prayer.... And thus did the pious and saintly people: They meditated and concentrated on their prayers until they reached the level of transcending physicality and elevating the power of the mind until they reached near the level of prophecy. (*Orah Hayyim*, 91)

The essential goal of *deveikut* is to feel close to God, to develop a sort of intimacy in which God's presence is a reality. Rabbi Aryeh Kaplan in his book *Jewish Meditation* offers a keen observation:

If you have experienced closeness to God even once in your life, then when I speak about God, you know exactly what I mean, and the concept has a very strong spiritual connotation. But if you have never had this experience, then God is something very abstract and can be described only on an intellectual level.... One who has never been in love might argue that love does not exist. The same is true of one who has never experienced God. But for one who has had the experience, there is no question.[2]

The Torah teaches that God created human beings in God's image (Genesis 1:27). Sages have offered their interpretations of what this phrase might mean. Some have suggested that God's image is manifested in the intellect, in free will, or in human creativity.

I gained an insight about the meaning of this phrase during the first Gulf War in the early 1990s. The United States had developed "smart missiles," which were capable of homing in on their targets. Even if the target made evasive moves, the "smart missiles" could readjust their course so that they would hit the target. It struck me that the "image of God" operates like a "smart missile." The Almighty implanted within human beings an innate drive to come closer to God. Even if God seems distant or seems to hide from us, our inner light impels us toward the Divine. We are programmed with a spiritual drive; if we allow it to flourish, we reach our goal (or at least come as close as possible). It is natural for us to be spiritual and to strive for spiritual fulfillment. Only if we suppress the "image of God" within us will we fail to strive toward God and godliness.

Maintaining Spiritual Balance

Draw me, we will run after you.

(SONG OF SONGS 1:4)

As discussed earlier in this book, the Talmud informs us that four sages entered the *pardes*, the realm of mystical speculation, and only Rabbi Akiva emerged in peace. The Talmud states:

> Rabbi Akiva ascended in peace and returned in peace. About him, the Bible states, "Draw me, we will run after you." Even in the case of Rabbi Akiva, the ministering angels sought to repel him [from the upper reaches of spiritual knowledge]. The Holy One blessed be He said: "Leave this elder alone. He is worthy to experience My honor [*lehishtamesh bikhvodi*]." (*Hagigah* 16a)

Rabbi Akiva felt overwhelmingly drawn to the Divine. He was impatient to rise higher and higher; he "ran" after God. The angels felt that Rabbi Akiva was reaching too far into the world of spirituality. God, though, informed the angels that Rabbi Akiva was worthy to rise to the heights. He had the capacity to absorb spiritual truths without losing his earthly balance.

His three other colleagues did not fare well in their visit to the *pardes*. Even great sages cannot easily blend the claims of the soul and the claims of the body. According to one interpretation, Ben Azzai did not literally die after his experience in the *pardes*. Rather, he continued to live in an otherworldly manner. He devoted himself entirely to spirit, becoming a spiritual ascetic, not marrying, engaging as little as possible in the business and needs of earthly existence.[1]

The ideal spirituality of Rabbi Akiva is difficult to attain. Some, like Ben Azzai, are so caught up in the spiritual quest that they

145

become otherworldly recluses. Others, like Ben Zoma and Rabbi Elisha ben Avuya, become so confused that they lose their sense of spiritual direction altogether.

The Talmud relates the story of Rabbi Shimon bar Yohai and his son Rabbi Elazar (*Shabbat* 33b–34a). The Roman authorities considered Rabbi Shimon to be a dangerous rebel, and they put out a death warrant for him. Rabbi Shimon and his son went into hiding in a cave. They survived by the miraculous appearance of a spring of water and a carob tree. During their twelve years in hiding, they studied and prayed all day and reached the pinnacle of mystical study and observance. After these twelve years of isolation, they received word that the Roman authorities had canceled the decree of death on Rabbi Shimon.

The two sages emerged from the cave and soon saw men plowing and sowing their fields. Rabbi Shimon was outraged: "They forsake eternal life and busy themselves with temporal life!" The Talmud then states, "Every place they turned their eyes was immediately burned. A heavenly voice came out and said to them: 'Did you leave [the cave] in order to destroy My world? Go back to the cave!'" After living in the pristine spiritual world of the cave, these two sages could not make peace with the mundane world. Everything they saw "burned up," that is, was consumed by their otherworldly passion. They could not understand why farmers plowed their fields instead of devoting themselves to the eternal life of the spirit. God chastised the sages. They returned to their cave for another year, as though they were being sentenced to punishment for being sinners.

At the conclusion of the twelve months, they again emerged from the cave. "Wherever Rabbi Elazar smote, Rabbi Shimon healed." Rabbi Elazar was evidently still not able to make peace with this worldly life. Rabbi Shimon sought to rectify his son's overzealousness. The Talmud continues:

> When the eve of the Sabbath arrived, they saw an old man holding two bunches of myrtle, running at twilight. They said to him, "Why do you need these?" He replied, "To honor the Sabbath." They said, "Would not one suffice

for you?" He said, "One for 'Remember [the Sabbath]' and one for 'Observe [the Sabbath].'" Since the Torah states that we are to remember and observe the Sabbath, this old man took two bunches of myrtle to welcome the Sabbath. Rabbi Shimon was deeply impressed. He told his son: "See how dear is a commandment to Israel." Rabbi Elazar's mind was set at ease.

The pious old man, in his love of the commandments to remember and observe the Sabbath, provided the sages with a new perspective on life in this world. We reach full spiritual fulfillment not by isolating ourselves in caves, but by keeping the commandments of the Torah with joy. Since the commandments are from the Almighty, they provide us with a means of fulfilling God's will in this world, thus allowing our souls the spiritual satisfaction of serving the Almighty with joy. As we "run after" the commandments, so our souls are "running" closer to God.

Illusions and Reality

> I am black but comely.... Look not upon me that I am
> swarthy, that the sun has tanned me.
>
> (SONG OF SONGS 1:5–6)

In these verses, the beautiful maiden apologizes for her swarthy appearance. She has been compelled to work as a shepherdess, spending long hours in the sun. Her skin has become deeply tanned and darkened. The fair maidens of the palace live in luxury in a protected environment; their skin is fair and untarnished. The maiden says: You may think that I am deficient in comparison with the courtly maidens, but do not judge my beauty by my external appearance. I am swarthy but beautiful.

The Midrash (*Song of Songs Rabbah* 1:5) elaborates on this theme: Externally, Torah sages may appear to be downtrodden and poor in appearance; yet internally, they are filled with Torah wisdom. Neither individuals nor groups should be judged by external standards.

The Talmud (*Pesahim* 50a) tells a remarkable story. The great sage Rabbi Yehoshua ben Levi had a promising and learned son who took ill and appeared to have died. The grief at the loss of this young man was immeasurable. But then, amazingly, the son revived. And the joy at his coming back to life was no doubt even greater than the grief at his supposed death.

Rabbi Yehoshua realized that his son had undergone a unique experience, having tasted death but then having been returned to life. So the father asked the son: What did you see on the other side? What is the nature of the world after death? The son responded: *Olam hafukh ra-iti*, I saw a topsy-turvy world. Those who are great here are small there; and those who are small here are

148

great there. Rabbi Yehoshua told his son: *Olam barur ra-ita*, you saw a clear world; you saw things the way they really are.

In this world, we live in the mist of illusions and shadows, and we are easily deceived. How can we know the real essence of anyone, if they are truly great or not, if they are truly good or not? How can we see things here as they ultimately are seen in the eyes of God? Only in the next world, the world of spirit and truth, does clarity prevail. In this world, not only are we not able to clearly understand others, but we often have difficulty even evaluating our own true selves.

Some people seem ordinary, and yet they are in fact extraordinary. Other people seem extraordinary, and yet they are in fact even less than ordinary. Wise people seek to avoid illusions and delusions about others ... and about themselves.

Looking after Our Spiritual Needs

They made me keeper of the vineyards, but my own vineyard I have not kept.

(SONG OF SONGS 1:6)

In *Pirkei Avot* (1:2), we read the opinion of the sage known as Shimon the Righteous: "The world stands on three foundations: on
the Torah, on divine worship, and on acts of loving-kindness." In
my commentary on this passage, I wrote:

> Torah represents a person's efforts at self-perfection; it
> entails study, introspection and a commitment to train
> oneself in the ways of righteousness. Divine worship
> represents a person's yearning for relationship with the
> Almighty. Through worship, one sees life in the con-
> text of the divine; one transcends the limited and limit-
> ing boundaries of the mundane. Acts of loving-kindness
> represent a person's interrelationship with other human
> beings. The goal of life is not to be a recluse, but to par-
> ticipate generously in the well-being of others.[1]

These three foundations are the sine qua non of a spiritually healthy
life. Yet, people often find themselves so busy that they do not focus
adequately on strengthening these foundations in their own lives.
They become so involved in day-to-day responsibilities that they
forget to tend their own spiritual vineyard.

How much time each day do we devote to Torah study and
introspection? How much effort do we expend in order to come
closer to the Almighty? What acts of genuine loving-kindness do we
perform each day, selflessly and generously?

150

The usual claim is that we do not have time for these things. Life's pressures are such that we need to spend many hours each day to earn our livings. When we do have free time, we feel that we are entitled to use it for recreation and pleasure, to relax from our busy lives. People will spend many hours traveling to and attending a sports event but claim not to have thirty minutes a day for study and reflection. They will wake up early to read the newspapers and business news but say they are not able to devote twenty minutes to prayer. They will spend hours watching television but indicate that they have no time to visit an ailing friend in the hospital or to volunteer at the local soup kitchen to feed the homeless.

Erich Fromm has noted:

> Most people fail in the art of living not because they are inherently bad or so without will that they cannot live a better life; they fail because they do not wake up and see when they stand at a fork in the road and have to decide.[2]

Put another way, we fail because we do not have the internal discipline to live according to a clear philosophy of life. Instead of making decisions that will keep us on track, we drift through life in a semipassive manner.

Sometimes our failures are the result of well-intentioned actions. We want to be good parents, good neighbors, and good citizens. We devote much time and energy to helping others fulfill their goals. In the process, though, we might lose focus on our own needs. We forget that we need to tend our own vineyards. Unless we are spiritually strong, we cannot live at our best. We then not only fail ourselves, but we also fail the very people we most want to help.

Think Carefully, Avoid Charlatans

If you know not, O you fairest among women, go your
way forth by the footsteps of the flock and feed your kids
beside the shepherds' tents.

(SONG OF SONGS 1:8)

In his novel *The Castle*, Franz Kafka describes the dilemma of a land
surveyor who believes he has been engaged by the castle to do some
work. But the land surveyor, known simply as K, arrives in the village
and sees the castle only in the distance. The way from the village to
the castle is labyrinthine, and K tries various unsuccessful strategies
to reach his goal. At some point, K is sharply rebuked by his landlady
in the village: "You are not from the castle, you are not from the village, you aren't anything."[1]

K's existential problem is that he does not seem to belong any-
where, and therefore he isn't anything. He is intelligent, he is a professional land surveyor, he has ingenuity and imagination; and yet,
K is lost between the worlds of the castle and the village. He has no
home to call his own, no base of operation where he is comfortable
and in control.

The dilemma of K can be extrapolated to a more general human
malaise. Some people seek spiritual fulfillment but do not know
where they belong. They are not part of a thriving religious community, and they are not drawn to the various kabbalists and gurus
who seek to win them over. The cries of "spirituality" are ubiquitous, but how is one to distinguish between an authentic religious
guide and a con artist who is nothing but a charlatan?

Unfortunately, there is no shortage of charismatic charlatans and
wonder-workers who prey on gullible, searching souls. Here is an

important piece of advice: steer clear of authoritarian, obscurantist teachers who claim to have a direct line to the Almighty.

Some people say: I'll find my own way. And some succeed at this. But imagine a person who wishes to become a musician and decides to find her own way without studying the earlier masters. Yes, this person might become a great musician, but most who follow this path will fail. They would be far better served if they first learned music from the musical geniuses of the past. Once they can play and fully understand Mozart and Beethoven, they can then develop their own talents with a firm baseline of musical expertise.

In his commentary on the Song of Songs, Rabbi Moshe Almosnino offers an interpretation of verse 1:8: if you do not know your way and you are confused about how to move ahead, follow the well-trodden tracks and rely upon the true and sturdy shepherds.[2] When you are not sure of the best way to proceed, you need not flail about helplessly. You should not simply follow your intuition as to what the best path is. Rather, it is best to fasten yourself to the tradition, to follow the well-trodden path of your religious predecessors. In the Jewish tradition, for example, we have many rites and traditions that provide a baseline of religious experience. We have thousands of years of wisdom produced by our spiritual shepherds going back to biblical times and all the way to our own day.

Once we have immersed ourselves in the spiritual treasures of our tradition, we can find internal strength and insight to help us along the journey of life. It is very helpful if we have the guidance of truly spiritual, truly honest, and truly good teachers. *Pirkei Avot* instructs us, "Get for yourself a teacher" (1:6). It is essential to find a spiritual guide who inspires us, educates us, and allows us to grow.

Authenticity

Behold you are beautiful, my love; behold you are beautiful; your eyes are as doves.

(Song of Songs 1:15)

The Midrash on this verse (*Song of Songs Rabbah* 1:15) interprets it
in a spiritual sense:

> Behold you are beautiful in [the fulfillment of the] mitz-
> voth, behold you are beautiful in acts of loving-kindness,
> behold you are beautiful in [fulfilling] the positive com-
> mandments, behold you are beautiful in [fulfilling] the
> negative commandments.

The Midrash is pointing to an important truth: a person's real
worth is determined by quality of character, not by external signs of
beauty. As Solomon stated in the concluding passages of Proverbs
(31:30), "Grace is deceitful and beauty is vain; but a woman who
fears the Lord, she shall be praised."

While it seems so obvious that people should be judged by their
goodness and integrity, it often happens that this is not the case.
Advertisers know that a beautiful image sells; they know that most
people are swayed by external appearances and rarely have the
time—or take the time—to evaluate things more carefully. In a society that is imbued with superficial surface relationships, people seek
a quick thrill or a moment of sensual pleasure; physical beauty is
highly emphasized.

The problem goes beyond physical beauty. It manifests itself in all
areas of life, where images are often more important than realities.
People go to great lengths to market themselves to gain popularity, clients, fame, and fortune. In the process, truth and dignity are

trampled. Without realizing it, society sinks into an idolatrous mental framework. Idolatry, at root, is a lie. It purports to limit God to a physical image. It has people worship an image—but not the real God. It focuses on physical image, not on eternal spirit.

In the 1956 film *The Invasion of the Body Snatchers*, invaders replace human beings with duplicates that appear identical on the surface but are devoid of any emotion or individuality. To the outside, everything looks the same. The physical bodies are still intact, but the souls are gone. This is, at core, the way of idolatry: to maintain an outward, physical appearance, while destroying connection with the inner soul. It worships form, not essence; it highlights external appearances, not inner spirit.

The nature of idolatry is manifested not only in worshiping statues. It also shows itself whenever people substitute external appearances for inner realities, when people go for glitz rather than essence, when they judge themselves and others by external appearances rather than by inner values. When people sell out truth for the sake of gaining popularity or power, they are actually engaging in idolatrous behavior.

What is the antidote to the disease of idolatry? If the hallmark of idolatry is falsehood and attachment to physical appearances, the antidote must be truth and the attachment to spiritual realities. The antidote is the proper understanding of our relationship with God, the source of absolute truth.

Rabbi Abraham Joshua Heschel, in an address to the Rabbinical Assembly in 1953, discussed a problem: even when people attend the synagogue on the Sabbath—and hence should be very much tuned in to a spiritual experience—they still might not internalize the religious message. Here is an excerpt from that talk:

> Of course, people still attend "services"—but what does this attendance mean to them? Outpouring of the soul? Worship? Prayer? Synagogue attendance has become a benefaction to the synagogue, a service to the community rather than service of God, worship of the congregation rather than the worship of God. A variety of suggestions

have been made to increase synagogue attendance: invite distinguished guest speakers, radio commentators and columnists; honor individual members of the congregation; install stained-glass windows, place pledge cards on the seats and raise funds, remind people of their birthdays or anniversary dates. Well intentioned as these suggestions may be, they do not deal with the core of the issue. Spiritual issues cannot be solved by administrative techniques. The issue is not how to fill buildings but how to inspire hearts. The issue is not synagogue attendance but one of spiritual attendance. The issue is not how to attract bodies to enter the space of a temple but how to inspire souls to enter an hour of spiritual concentration in the presence of God.[1]

In its ongoing battle against idolatry, Judaism seeks to focus our minds and souls on authenticity and truth. Our religious lives and our religious institutions must not lose authenticity and truth by succumbing to the shallowness and hollowness of a "showbiz" mentality.

It is possible for something to look beautiful on the outside but to be empty on the inside. It is possible to maintain the appearance of success while, in fact, having lost one's soul. The price of idolatry is very high, too high.[2]

The Courage to Stand Alone

As a lily among thorns, so is my love among the daughters.

(SONG OF SONGS 2:2)

The Midrash (*Song of Songs Rabbah* 2:2) quotes Rabbi Yitzhak, who applied this verse to our matriarch Rebecca: "Her father was a deceiver, her brother was a deceiver, and the people of her place were deceivers; and yet this righteous woman arose from among them like a lily among thorns." The larger meaning is that a person has the power to overcome environmental pressures. But to do so, one must have spiritual courage, the ability to stand alone against the crowd.

In his classic work *The Lonely Man of Faith*, Rabbi Joseph B. Soloveitchik writes of two aspirations of human beings: dignity and redemption.[1] Dignity results whenever we triumph over nature—for example, when we make scientific and technological advances, when we control our environment, when we achieve social or economic success. In these instances, we see ourselves as masters, not as victims. This is dignity.

Redemption, though, is something quite different. It stems not from our feeling of being in control but from our feeling of being entirely dependent on God. We are vulnerable. We are afraid. We recognize deeply and without reservation that our lives are in God's hands, not our own. No matter how successful we may appear to be, only God has full control. Rabbi Soloveitchik notes that dignity is discovered at the summit of success; redemption in the depth of crisis and failure.

Put into other terms, dignity can be described in our résumés. We can list our achievements, honors, titles, our material assets.

But redemption is something deep within us that we cannot quite explain to others. It is not quantifiable.

The dynamic inner life of a religious person attempts to balance the human need for dignity with the equally human need for redemption. It does not ignore the claims of the material world but also does not forget our soul, our ultimate purpose in life. This tension leads to the courage to stand alone courageously, to be different and not to follow blindly the passing fads and trends of society.

Our forefather Abraham exemplifies the classic loner. God commanded him to leave his land, his birthplace, his father's home—and to set off in a new direction, to a new land, to a new society. Abraham was to spread his revolutionary notion of one God and a system of ethical monotheism.

The Torah makes clear that Abraham was a man of dignity. He had wealth and a coterie of followers. He could muster troops to wage and win military battles. He had an impressive résumé of achievements and material successes. But the Torah also makes clear that Abraham was a man who sought redemption. He humbly followed God's commands, even at great personal sacrifice. He prayed to God and served God, recognizing that God's will—not his own—must prevail.

Abraham was a personality marked by profound courage. He was able to teach a new and grand idea, to foster a religious vision that made tremendous demands on the faithful. Abraham was known as *Ivri* (the Hebrew), and our Rabbis noted that the root of the word *Ivri* relates to being on the other side—the whole of society was on one side, and Abraham stood alone on the other side. Society could measure Abraham's material success and dignity, but his challenge was to make them understand the need for redemption, for inner spiritual transformation.

In this respect, Abraham set the agenda for his spiritual descendants. We are surely to work for the scientific, technological, and material benefit of humanity—to foster human dignity. But we have the far more difficult task of working for the spiritual advancement of humanity—to foster redemption. We need the heroism of Abraham to stand on one side, even if much of the world stands on the other side. We need to learn for ourselves so that we can teach others: material dignity is not enough for human salvation; we require spiritual depth, humility, a sense of living in the presence of God.

There is a midrash that teaches that when the Messiah is about to arrive, the Almighty will spread two bridges across the ocean. One will be made of steel and the other will be made of paper. Most will choose the steel bridge, but it will collapse. The righteous will choose the paper bridge and will arrive at redemption.

Steel symbolizes putting reliance on physical strength, wealth, power—the material signs of success and dignity. Paper symbolizes putting reliance on ideas, on our holy books. Strangely enough, it is the paper bridge that is actually stronger and that leads to redemption.

Rabbi Soloveitchik pointed out that the "lonely man of faith" is not lacking friends and social context. Rather, the loneliness is ontological, an essential ingredient in the human psyche. In spite of being surrounded by people, a person of faith has a yearning for the transcendent God. No one else outside of her can fully understand what is transpiring within her mind and heart and soul. This loneliness is not a negative quality but is at the root of spiritual growth.

Love of God

He has brought me to the banqueting-house, and his banner over me is love.

(SONG OF SONGS 2:4)

For some, the relationship with God is rooted in fear. They view God as a strict disciplinarian just waiting to mete out punishment to sinners. While such individuals may live moral and upright lives, they have difficulty coming close to God.

In his commentary on the Song of Songs, Rabbi Moshe Almosnino interprets "his banner over me is love" to mean that God primarily relates to humans through the quality of love.[1] As we draw closer to God, we realize that God is a loving and compassionate Parent who wants us to live happy and good lives.

The Torah teaches, "And you shall love the Lord your God with all your heart, and with all your soul, and with all your might" (Deuteronomy 6:5). The Talmud (*Berakhot* 54a) explains that "with all your heart" means that we must serve God with total commitment. Even our negative impulses should be redirected into positive ways to serve God. "With all your soul" means that we should be willing to suffer martyrdom for the sake of God.

"With all your might" is explained in several ways. It might mean that we should be willing to forfeit monetary assets in order to serve God properly. Or it might mean that we should love God in good times and bad. Even at moments of suffering and distress, we should muster the personal faith and wisdom to offer blessings to God.

Rabbi Adin Steinsaltz pointed out that the Hasidic master Rabbi Shneur Zalman of Liadi interpreted *bekhol me'odekha*, "with all your might," as follows:

In everything that one does, one must do more, in the sense of *me'od* which literally means "more." This understanding of *me'od* makes "with all your might" an even higher level than giving up one's life; giving up one's life requires a moment's decision, and with that the matter is settled, whereas "with all your might" ... represents unending love of God.[2]

The interpretation offered by Rabbi Shneur Zalman of Liadi calls on us to feel a genuine, ongoing love of God that prods us to do more, to yearn for a relationship with God at an ever closer level. This love is manifested in the everyday activities of life, in the daily struggles and challenges that we face. Love of God is not reserved for special high moments or sacred spaces; it is ever present. It is a deep, constant yearning within us.

The Yearnings of Love

For I am lovesick.

(Song of Songs 2:5)

To be lovesick is to be overcome with an aching longing. It is not the result of rational calculations, but of a powerful and all-consuming feeling of oneness with the beloved.

The Hebrew word for "love," *ahavah*, derives from the root letters *aleph-heh-vav*, meaning "to give." A loving person is motivated by a desire to give to the beloved, to sacrifice for the beloved. This is in radical contrast to the lustful person, whose goal is to exploit and to take. A loving relationship is characterized by a "we-consciousness," not a "me-consciousness." It is not about winning victories over the other, nor about negotiating favorable terms for the relationship; it is about viewing the world as a "we" rather than as an "I."

In my long career as a rabbi, I have met with many couples who were planning their marriages, and I have performed many weddings. While the vast majority of these couples were glowing with love, there were those who seemed to view marriage as just another business deal. What can I get out of this relationship? How will this marriage advance my goals? In one particular instance, I sensed that the person contemplating marriage seemed incapable of actually loving anyone. Perhaps she had been abused as a child. Perhaps she had developed serious mistrust of others due to negative experiences in her life. For her, marriage was a duty expected of her by her family, and she was doing it to fulfill a social obligation. She would gain some status, financial benefits, and a nice place to live. She would take what she could from the relationship, but her ability to give selflessly and lovingly was deficient.

162

It seems that being genuinely lovesick is becoming increasingly difficult in modern society. The emphasis is on "me," rather than on "us." Relationships are more tentative: let's see what I can get out of it, let's see how long it makes me happy. Many people are choosing not to get married or to defer marriage to a later age. A significant percentage of marriages are ending in divorce. The pervasive culture emphasizes personal satisfaction and sense of entitlement. What can others do for me? How can I shine more than others? Don't I deserve better?

The test of real love is not a passing infatuation or a temporary relationship that provides "me" with satisfaction. Rather, it is a long-term genuine commitment to a beloved person. David Brooks has well described the love of those who have made a deep lifelong commitment to one another. The person they

> once loved hotly they now love warmly but steadily, happily, unshakably. They don't even think of loving their beloved because they want something back. They just naturally offer love as a matter of course. It is gift-love, not reciprocity-love.[1]

The Song of Songs has traditionally been interpreted as an expression of lovesickness for God. We have a deep longing to feel a relationship with God. Rabbi Abraham Isaac Kook, in his poem "Expanses, Expanses," poured out his heart: "I am lovesick / I thirst, I thirst for God, / As a deer for water brooks. / Alas, who can describe my pain?"[2] The lover of God suffers from an unquenchable yearning to come near the Eternal and the Infinite.

Lovesickness for God is not the same as lovesickness for a beloved human being. While the lover wants to give, there is nothing that God needs from us. While the lover wants mutuality, it is impossible for a finite human being to have a mutual relationship with the Almighty Holy One.

Too often, those who profess love of God are in fact seeking something from God. They see God as the dispenser of health, wealth, miracles of all sorts. They think that if they worship God, they will be entitled to receive rewards from God. If/when they feel that God has not answered their prayers appropriately, they become upset or their faith is shaken.

But true lovesickness for God is selfless love. It emerges from the totality of who we are. It is an overwhelming thirst for transcendence. To be able to sense God's presence, even for an instant, is a blessing of cosmic proportions. The lovesick human being does not condition his love on what God can do for him.

The great eighteenth-century Hasidic master Rabbi Levi Yitzhak of Berdichev described the true love of God as being in the realm of "face to face," a direct and complete love that seeks union with God without expectation of external benefits. To serve God with ulterior motives is an inferior level of religiosity (*Kedushat Levi*, on Genesis 32:31).

The ancient sage Antigonos of Soho taught, "Do not be like servants who serve their master on condition of receiving a reward, but be like servants who serve their master not on condition of receiving a reward" (*Pirkei Avot* 1:3).

Truth and Compassion

Let his left hand be under my head and his right hand embrace me.

(SONG OF SONGS 2:6)

In kabbalistic literature, the "left" is identified with the quality of *gevurah*, "strength" or "heroism." The "right" is identified with *hesed*, "compassion" or "kindness." Both qualities are needed for a balanced life.

Gevurah entails a courageous commitment to truth. The Talmud (*Taanit* 4a) cites the opinion of Rav Ashi that "any Torah scholar who is not hard as iron is no Torah scholar!" What he meant was that a rabbi must have strong principles, must be courageous in upholding these principles, and must not bend under pressure. This statement applies to all people, not just Torah scholars. In a world where so many individuals adopt artificial and false personae to impress others, we need the strength to be genuine, to stand for truth even if we must stand alone.

Shortly after Rav Ashi's statement, the Talmud cites the opinion of Ravina: "Even so, a person must teach himself the quality of gentleness." While it is vital to be strong in our principles, it is equally important to be gentle. We teach not by threatening or coercing, but by exuding a spirit of love, kindness, and gentleness.

While the "left hand" should be under my head—a steady reminder to adhere to truth—the "right hand" should embrace me—should be the dominant feature of my personality. We are obliged to live a courageous and disciplined life, but our actions and thoughts must be tempered by a spirit of compassion and empathy for others. Religion that overly stresses discipline and truth becomes judgmental and intolerant. It can become ugly and dangerous, even to the extent of fostering cruelty, violence, and murder of those who are considered dissenters or enemies of faith.

A midrash relates that when the Almighty was about to create Adam, a debate broke out among the angels. Some advised God not to create human beings; others urged their creation. *Hesed* (compassion) said, "Let human beings be created because they will do acts of kindness." *Emet* (truth) said, "Let them not be created because they will be filled with lies." *Tzedek* (righteousness) said, "Create them because they will do acts of justice." *Shalom* (peace) said, "Don't create them because they will be filled with strife."

God then cast *Emet* down to earth. The angels objected, "Why did you treat *Emet* disrespectfully, since truth is Your hallmark?" God replied, "The truth will blossom forth from the earth."

And then Adam was created.

At the very point of the creation of humanity, this midrash teaches, it was clear that human beings would be a mixed blessing. They would form a society filled with lies and strife—but also filled with compassion and peace. In weighing the pluses and minuses, God opted for creating humanity. God planted truth into the soil of the earth, with the confidence that one day truth will blossom, and humanity will be redeemed.

In Rabbinic tradition, Moses is identified with truth, and Aaron is identified with compassion. God chose to give commandments through both of them. If Moses was often strong and demanding, Aaron was often resilient and kind. Moses and Aaron represent two essential qualities—truth and compassion—which together can tilt humanity in the right direction.

There has long been a dissonance between our inner world of truth and compassion and the external world in which we live, a world in which lies and violence abound. Throughout the ages, Jews have been subjected to one persecution after another; every sort of lie has been lodged against us; we have been maligned and murdered generation after generation. We look around at our world today and see that repressive nations are given seats of honor at the United Nations—and Israel is routinely condemned! We see terrorist regimes threatening Israel, firing missiles into Israel—and yet the world faults Israel consistently. We see anti-Semitic lies go unchallenged, we see terrorism against Jews idealized, we see a world full of "good people" who stand by and do nothing or say nothing in defense of the Jewish people.

And yet, we persist in our inner spiritual world. We say our prayers each day. We maintain faith in God and in the ultimate redemption of humanity. Our faith in God is remarkable, but our faith in humanity is even more remarkable. After all we have experienced, can we really believe that people will change for the better or that their hatred, lies, and violence will come to an end?

The figure of Moses reminds us that we cannot compromise in our search for truth. We cannot shy away from the demand for genuine justice. The figure of Aaron reminds us that we must not forget about human frailty and fear, we may not lose sight of compassion and peace. Jewish life—and human life in general—must be a dynamic process of thinking and growing and courageous commitment to those values that redound to the glory of humanity. When we see ugly behavior and hear ugly words around us, we realize how far humanity still falls short from fulfilling God's hopes for us.

God cast *Emet* to the earth, indicating that the day will surely come when truth will blossom forth, when individuals and nations will admit their lies and injustices and cruelties. On that day, all of humanity will be redeemed. Truth will become so clear that human beings will cleanse their souls and recognize the hand of God in their lives.

When we strive to internalize the teachings and characteristics of Moses and Aaron, we bring more truth and compassion into the world. In our day-to-day lives, these little steps may seem trivial in the face of the many problems confronting us and humanity. Yet in the cosmic struggle for the soul of humankind, we move the world a little closer to the day when truth will blossom forth from the earth.[1]

Setting God Before Us at All Times

Oh my dove, you are in the clefts of the rock, in the
covert of the cliff; let me see your countenance, let me
hear your voice; for sweet is your voice and your countenance is comely.

(SONG OF SONGS 2:14)

Rabbi Harold Kushner tells a story of a man who stopped attending his usual synagogue and was now frequenting another minyan.
One day he happened to meet the rabbi of his previous synagogue,
and the rabbi asked him where he was praying these days. The man
answered, "I am praying at a small minyan led by Rabbi Cohen."

The rabbi was stunned. "Why would you want to pray there with
that rabbi? I am a much better orator, I am more famous, I have a
much larger following."

The man replied, "Yes, but in my new synagogue the rabbi has
taught me to read minds."

The rabbi was surprised. "All right, then, read my mind."

The man said, "You are thinking of the verse in Psalms, 'I have
set the Lord before me at all times' [Psalm 16:8]."

"You are wrong," said the rabbi, "I was not thinking about that
verse at all."

The man replied, "Yes, I knew that, and that's why I've moved
to the other synagogue. The rabbi there is always thinking of this
verse."[1]

Indeed, an authentically religious person is always thinking of
this verse, either directly or in the back of his mind. Such an individual lives in the presence of God, conducts himself with modesty

and propriety. The Rabbi Cohen of the story was genuine; he was a spiritual person seeking to live a godly life.

The other rabbi in the story was outwardly successful. He had a large congregation and external signs of prestige. But he lacked the essential ingredient of being authentically religious: he did not have God before him at all times. He was busy trying to make himself popular, get his name into the newspapers, rub elbows with celebrities. Even when he prayed, his mind was not on God but on how he could advance himself in the world.

The founding father of Judaism (and ethical monotheism as a whole) was Abraham. The Torah does not describe Abraham as a great orator or statesman. Rather, he was one who walked before God, in the presence of God. God refers to Abraham as *ohavi*, "My friend" (Isaiah 41:8). Friendship implies a loving mutual relationship, loyalty, trustworthiness. Abraham was not a self-aggrandizing politician or a back-slapping smooth salesman.

Others in Abraham's time may have been mightier, more popular, and wealthier. But God chose Abraham because Abraham was true. Abraham was the one who would become "father of a multitude of nations." Abraham was the one who would ultimately prevail in bringing the world closer to God and closer to godliness.

Our goal should be to set God before us at all times and to associate with others who strive to do likewise. Life is too important to waste by clinging to falseness and vanity.

Spiritual Spoilers

The foxes take hold of us, the little foxes that spoil the
vineyards.

(SONG OF SONGS 2:15)

Who are the "foxes" who spoil—or attempt to spoil—our spiritual
development?

Some are "foxes" from the outside. They contribute to the intel-
lectual/cultural climate that fosters atheism, agnosticism, excessive
rationalism. They scorn the religious adventure, seeing it as a means
of controlling the unthinking masses.

Some are "foxes" from the inside. They pose as religious guides,
but they foster an authoritarian, obscurantist, and fundamentalist
approach to spirituality. They prey on gullible souls and draw them
into cults or cult-like communities. They insist that people follow
them blindly, and they punish those who do not do so.

Some are "foxes" from within our own minds. We ask ourselves:
If we devote time to prayer and meditation, will our family and
friends think that we are strange? If we take religious life seriously,
will we lose credibility with the freethinkers among whom we live?
If we pride ourselves on our rationalism, can we really embrace a
spirituality that transcends reason? Our self-doubts make us insecure, even fearful.

"Foxes" often are able to "spoil our vineyards" because we do
not have a clear idea of the nature of religious/spiritual life. Too
often, religion is perceived as a form of irrational superstition. Yet,
true religion and true spirituality are the opposite of—and opposed
to—superstition.

In my book *Maimonides, Spinoza and Us*, I discuss a Maimoni-
dean approach to religion and superstition.[1] Judaism seeks to bring

us closer to God through proper thought and deed. Superstition seeks to circumvent God's power through the use of magical formulas or rituals. Judaism demands intellectual and moral excellence and a direct relationship with God; superstition provides purported means of bypassing or manipulating God to ward off evil or to achieve some other desired goal.

The Torah is emphatic in commanding that we not turn to shamans or wonder-workers, but that we stay focused on our personal relationship with God:

> There shall not be found among you anyone ... who uses divination, a soothsayer, or an enchanter, or a sorcerer, or a charmer, or one who consults a ghost or a familiar spirit, or a necromancer. For whoever does these things is an abomination unto the Lord. (Deuteronomy 18:10–12)

Maimonides clarifies the boundaries between religion and superstition in his discussion about using incantations to heal a wound:

> Anyone who whispers a charm over a wound and reads a verse from the Torah, or one who recites a biblical verse over a child lest he be terrified, or one who places a Torah scroll or tefillin over an infant to enable him to sleep, are not only included in the category of sorcerers and charmers, but are included among those who repudiate the Torah. They use the words of the Torah as a physical cure, whereas they are exclusively a cure for the soul, as it is written, "They will be life to your soul" [Proverbs 3:22]. On the other hand, one who is enjoying good health is permitted to recite biblical verses, or a psalm, that he may be shielded and saved from affliction and damage by virtue of the reading. (*Mishneh Torah*, Laws of Idolatry 11:12)

What are the characteristics of those individuals who "repudiate the Torah"? (1) They treat biblical verses as though they are magic formulas that can effect a cure. (2) They use religious objects (e.g., Torah scroll, tefillin), as though they are endowed with independent magical powers. (3) They resort to incantations and magical rituals rather than turning directly to God. In short, they behave superstitiously, rather than religiously.

These individuals might well think of themselves as being pious, Torah-true Jews. After all, they have not gone to soothsayers or diviners for help; they have recited the holy words of the Bible and have used religious items of our own Jewish tradition. Wherein have they sinned? Maimonides would answer: to use the Torah's words and symbols in a superstitious way is also superstition!

Maimonides notes that if a healthy person chants biblical verses in the hope that the merit of this mitzvah will invite God's protection, this is still on the correct side of the line separating religion from superstition. The person is not attributing intrinsic supernatural power to the biblical verses; rather, she is directing her thoughts to God and hopes that the merit of her biblical readings will engender God's protection. Although this may not be an example of religion at its best, it is permissible—and not in the category of repudiating the Torah.

What leads people to superstitious behavior? Why doesn't everyone realize the foolishness of employing magical incantations and rites? Why would people rely on superstitious behavior rather than turning directly to God with their prayers?

Here are a few reasons:

1. True religion demands a lot from us. Superstition demands very little. True religion requires that we confront God directly. Superstition offers shortcuts, ways to bypass that awe-inspiring confrontation with God.
2. Superstitious practices have been sanctioned by generations of people who seem to have religious credibility. If these great ones believed in demons and made amulets, then these things must be permissible.
3. When people are afraid and desperate, they may suspend their reason in order to adopt superstitious practices just in case these might be efficacious. Why take chances by not trying everything?

A great challenge for religious leadership today is to wean people from superstitious tendencies and bring them closer to God. People need to be reminded to use their reason, rather than to surrender to a mindless supernaturalism. Religion teaches responsibility, careful thinking, and reliance on God. Superstition promotes avoidance of personal responsibility, suspension of rational thinking, and reliance on supernatural forces other than God.

Seeking to live a spiritual life "in love with God" does not at all mean surrendering reason or personal responsibility. On the contrary, succumbing to blind obedience to cult or cult-like leaders is dangerous spiritually and, too often, may lead to physical and financial abuse.

Hitbodedut—Meditation

By night on my bed I sought him whom my soul loves;
I sought him, but I did not find him. I will rise now and
go about the city, in the streets and in the broad ways, I
will seek him whom my soul loves. I sought him, but I
found him not.

(Song of Songs 3:1–2)

In the opening pages of his book *The Upright Thinkers*, Dr. Leonard Mlodinow reports an incident in his father's life as an inmate in a Nazi concentration camp.[1] The elder Mlodinow was then a young Polish Jew who had not received formal education past seventh grade. In the camp, he met an older inmate, a mathematician, and they struck up a friendship.

At some point, the mathematician posed a math problem to Mlodinow. The latter struggled to solve the problem but could not do so. He asked the mathematician for the answer. But the mathematician held back, telling the young man to keep trying. After several more days of agonizing over the problem, the young man still could not solve it, so he asked for the answer. The mathematician replied: I'll give you the answer only if you pay me by giving me the crust of bread that is your daily sustenance. The young Mlodinov handed over his bread and was given the solution to the math problem.

In recounting this story about his father, Dr. Mlodinow cites this as a classic example of the human desire for knowledge. His father was ready to give up his meager food ration in order to learn the answer to a math problem that made no practical difference in his life. Yet, his mind—like the best human minds—was willing to sacrifice much for the sake of attaining knowledge and truth.

Just as there is a deep human desire to attain knowledge, so there is a deep desire to experience the Divine. We would be willing to give our last crust of bread for the Answer, for a luminous moment when we are certain that we are in the presence of God. But, often enough, we may feel that we have sought Him but found Him not.

Striving for God, even when we fail to feel God's presence, is a sign that we are spiritually alive. Relationship with God is not a status that is attained and then remains forever in place. Rather, it is a dynamic process with ongoing fluctuations. At times, we feel that God is closer to us than we are to ourselves. At other times, we feel a frightening absence of God in our lives.

Loving God in good times and bad is a spiritual goal to which we should aspire. But there are times when we—like Pip in *Moby Dick*—feel lost at sea, lost and abandoned.

Jewish tradition provides ongoing entryways for us as we seek the presence of the Divine. The many positive and negative laws and customs of the *halakha* (Jewish law) are intended to bring us closer to God on a regular basis. If we fulfill the laws with proper intention (*kavanah*), then we are thinking of God almost constantly. Traditionally, we make at least one hundred blessings each day—during prayer, before and after eating, when fulfilling various mitzvoth. Each of these blessings provides a spiritual moment, an opening to the Almighty.

One of the virtues stressed by Jewish ethical teachers and kabbalists is *hitbodedut*, making time to be alone. Rabbi Aryeh Kaplan defines this term as meditation. The great Hasidic master Rav Nachman of Breslov (1772–1810) taught that *hitbodedut* is the best and highest level of worship:

> Set aside an hour or more each day to meditate, in the fields or in a room, pouring out your thoughts to God. Make use of arguments and persuasion, with words of grace, longing and petition, supplicating God and asking that He bring you to serve Him in truth.[2]

Rav Nachman suggested that we speak to God regularly, using our own natural language and expressing our sincere feelings.

> This is a very great practice. It is the best possible advice, including all things. It is good for everything that may be lacking in your relationship with God. Even if you are completely removed from God, you should still express your thoughts to Him and ask [that He bring you back].³

At times, we feel that we call out for God but "find Him not." We feel spiritually blocked. Rav Nachman teaches that even at such moments, we should speak to God. The very act of speaking naturally and sincerely is a way of finding the way back into a living relationship with the Almighty.

"Create a pure heart within me, O God, and renew within me an upright spirit; do not cast me away from Your presence, and do not take from me Your holy spirit" (Psalm 51:12–13).

Shalom—In Search of Wholeness

Behold, it is the litter of Solomon; sixty mighty men are around it, of the mighty men of Israel. They all handle the sword and are expert in war; every man has his sword upon his thigh because of fear of the night.

(SONG OF SONGS 3:7–8)

The Midrash (*Song of Songs Rabbah* 3:7) interprets the "sixty mighty men" of this verse to refer to the sixty letters in the Priestly Blessing (Numbers 6:24–26). That blessing calls upon God to bless and guard us; to shine God's countenance upon us and be gracious to us; to lift God's countenance on us and grant us peace. If we enjoy these blessings, then we can overcome "fear of the night," that is, fear of lurking dangers. We can live with a sense of well-being.

Even a powerful and wise person like King Solomon had fears and insecurities. He needed sixty of the mighty men of Israel to protect him. The Midrash interprets "of the mighty men" to mean that these men conveyed strength to Solomon. They encouraged him and gave him confidence to overcome his inner doubts.

Many people feel the need to be noticed. They dye their hair neon green, or they wear immodest clothing, or they say things that are intended to shock. They will do anything to keep the limelight focused on themselves: they will tell a stream of jokes, they will speak without listening to others, they will take "selfies" and send them to anyone and everyone they can think of. The message they convey is: *Notice me!*

Underlying this thirst for attention is the deep feeling of unworthiness, the fear of not being noticed. Also underlying this exhibitionism is the desire to stand above the crowd, to be distinguished in some way from the normal run of humanity.

Human beings are often (always?) frail and insecure. They need to be reassured that their lives mean something to others. They dread being ignored or forgotten. It is as though they evaluate the worthiness of their lives by how others respond to them. Their feelings of success or failure in life are determined by others.

The ancient Chinese philosopher Confucius taught, "What the Noble Person seeks is in himself. What the petty person seeks is in others." The challenge is to be the Noble Person.

The Torah commands the priests to be the conduits of blessing to the people of Israel. The culmination of the blessing states, "May God shine His countenance upon you and give you *shalom*" (Numbers 6:26).

Shalom, usually translated as "peace," has the connotation of wholeness. The blessing is recited in the singular (*lekha*, not *lakhem*), meaning that it is aimed at each particular person, not at the people at large. The blessing is for each of us as individuals to feel a sense of completeness within ourselves, to feel secure and unafraid. The blessing is to understand that the value of our lives is dependent on ourselves, not on the opinions of others. When the Almighty shines God's countenance upon each of us, we come to understand that life is ultimately defined by the relationship of ourselves with God. God's light eliminates the shadows and doubts.

Rabbi Ovadia Seforno, the great medieval Italian Jewish Bible commentator, notes one of the lessons to be derived from the Priestly Blessing: "May [God] enlighten your eyes with the light of His countenance, so that you will see wonders in His Torah and His creations."[1]

The blessing is for us to experience the divine light so that we can truly see and see truly; so that we can find enlightenment and excitement in our study and observance of Torah; so that we can look on God's creations with thoughtfulness and spiritual uplift. In our quest for personal wholeness, we need to see the world—and ourselves—with wise and thoughtful eyes.

God's Name Is Truth

Your lips are like a thread of scarlet and your mouth is comely.

(SONG OF SONGS 4:3)

Rabbi Moshe Almosnino takes this verse as a reference to the virtue of speaking truth.[1] He applies it to the people of Israel, who love God with a total love and who cling to truth, since God insists on truth. They conduct themselves with humility and justice, never forgetting

In George Orwell's novel *1984*, we are introduced to a frightening fictional world that may evolve into the real world of the future. It is a world based on lies. The three slogans of the ruling party are "War Is Peace; Freedom Is Slavery; Ignorance Is Strength."[2] Through manipulation of people's minds, through ruthless and persistent brainwashing, and through shameless rewriting of history, the ruling party creates a frightened and dehumanized society.

We have not yet arrived at Orwell's nightmare of a world, but aspects of his fears surely are evident. In totalitarian societies, the ruling party dictates what people may and may not know. Propaganda replaces the honest search for truth. Dissidents are imprisoned, tortured, or murdered. Some societies are controlled by a religious totalitarianism. The religious leaders demand total allegiance; they incite their followers to commit acts of terrorism and murder, even to become suicide bombers. They brook no dissent.

Even in free societies, falsehood finds easy access through our media, advertising, and publicity spinning. Public opinion is constantly manipulated by those who wish to advance their views; truth is not their primary concern.

U.S. Supreme Court justice Robert Jackson took leave from the court to serve as the U.S. chief prosecutor at the Nuremberg trials of Nazi war criminals. He wrote that "the most odious of all oppressions are those which mask as justice."[3] He sharply criticized the role of judges and legal systems to legitimize tyranny and oppression.

Judge Jackson understood that the atrocities of the Nazis were all purported to be legal. Laws were passed depriving Jews of all rights. Laws were passed to round up, imprison, and murder Jews. All those who participated in these heinous actions were following the law of the land!

The problem, though, was that the law itself was starkly immoral; the government that promulgated murderous laws was itself evil; the "legal system" that allowed such "laws" to be passed and implemented was the epitome of injustice, cruelty, and wickedness. Moral people should have denounced such "laws" and should have resisted the "legal system." If enough good people had risen against the tyrannical laws and the murderous Nazi regime, millions of lives would have been saved.

In our times, we also witness tendencies to legitimize wicked and immoral behavior by means of declaring such evil to be "legal." The United Nations is perhaps the world's most nefarious example of this tendency. The UN espouses resolutions and policies that are dressed in the garb of "international law" when in fact these resolutions and policies are classic examples of immorality, injustice, and corruption of the value of law. Orwell's fears of a world where lies become "truth" were not so far off the mark after all.

It's not just the UN that tends to cloak immorality in the dress of justice. There are groups of anti-Israel and anti-Semitic people who seek to undermine Israel; they insidiously pose as being interested in human rights, as guardians of international law. Yet, they operate with malice toward Israel and perpetrate the vilest propaganda against her; they support boycotts of Israel; they constantly rebuke Israel for any real or imagined shortcoming. For these people, justice is not just at all; rather they pervert justice to further their own unjust and immoral goals.

Psalm 81:10 reads, "Let there be no strange god among you." The Talmud (*Shabbat* 105b) offers a literal and profound interpretation of this phrase, reading it as "you shall not have within yourself a strange god." The verse is not warning us against worshiping external idols. Rather, it is telling us to look within ourselves for strange gods, for evil inclinations, for false divinities. It is demanding that we introspect, that we maintain truth, and that we reject the false gods that mislead us into erroneous beliefs and corrupt behaviors.[4]

It is interesting, and significant, that Orwell identified the greatest enemy of Big Brother and the totalitarian regime of *1984* by a stereotypical Jewish name: Emmanuel Goldstein. Orwell must have seen Jews as a singular hope for humanity, the one group that stands for freedom and mutual respect. Emmanuel Goldstein is vilified and hated by the ruling clique because he represents a worldview committed to truth, honesty, and justice. Emmanuel Goldstein, the persona of the Jewish people, terrifies oppressors. The eternal Jew is the eternal conscience of humanity. Bravo, Emmanuel Goldstein.

Being Awake to New Challenges

I sleep but my heart is awake; Hark, my beloved knocks....
I opened to my beloved, but my beloved had turned
away and was gone. My soul failed me when he spoke. I
sought him, but I could not find him; I called him but he
gave me no answer.

(SONG OF SONGS 5:2, 5:6)

I am my beloved's and my beloved is mine.

(SONG OF SONGS 6:3)

In 1956, Rabbi Joseph B. Soloveitchik delivered an address to the
Religious Zionists of America, which he entitled "*Kol Dodi Dofek*"
(Hark, My Beloved Knocks).[1] At that time, Jews were still reeling
in the staggering aftermath of the Holocaust; how were they to
cope with the wanton murder of six million Jews by the Nazis and
their accomplices? While they grieved in horror at the destruction of
European Jewry, they also were heartened by the rise of the State of
Israel in 1948.

Rabbi Soloveitchik noted that it was unproductive to try to
explain why the Holocaust happened or why evil persists in our
world. It is not fruitful to attempt to explain away evil by means of
artificial theodicies. God's mysteries remain beyond our ken. Rather,
the focus needs to be on the future. Now that we have suffered
pain and disaster, how are we to respond? How do we garner the
strength and courage to keep going, to rebuild, to reconstitute our
lives in the shadow of the valley of death?

Rabbi Soloveitchik, drawing on the imagery of the Song of Songs,
described the longings of the maiden who yearns to be reunited with

her beloved. She is in bed, unable to sleep. Her thoughts are on her beloved. Then, suddenly, she hears a knocking at the door. Her beloved has actually come to her home. At this very moment, when she should have eagerly sprung up from bed to open the door for him, the maiden becomes hesitant. She complains that she is tired. It would be uncomfortable to get up to go to the door. She hesitates while she hears the knocks on the door. At last, she decides to arise, but when she gets to the door, her beloved has already left. She is too late; she has missed her opportunity. She goes outside to search for him, she calls for him, she truly loves him; but he has come and gone away.

Rabbi Soloveitchik suggested that the maiden—that is, the people of Israel—longs to be united with God, the beloved. And yet, when God knocks at the door, Israel finds itself unable to go to the door and respond to this opportunity. Israel is tired, in pain. Israel has become numbed by its woes.

Rabbi Soloveitchik called on his audience to wake up to God's knocking on the door, to respond to the divine challenges of the moment. God was knocking; He was showing His hand in our history, demonstrating His ongoing love for us. God's knocking was revealed in the establishment of the State of Israel. After nearly two thousand years of exile, the Jewish people were returning to their ancient homeland. God was answering the prayers of so many generations of Jews who had yearned for their restoration to the Holy Land of their ancestors. Rabbi Soloveitchik challenged: The door is knocking, our beloved God is so very close to us. Are we responding with alacrity? Are we embracing this amazing opportunity for fulfilling and deepening our relationship of love?

Rabbi Soloveitchik thought that the religious Jewish community had not fully grasped the overwhelming significance of the moment. They did not adequately respond to God's knocking, God's prodding them to come forward, to embrace the new State of Israel with religious fervor and love.

We cannot erase the past tragedies that have befallen our people. But we can respond to the new challenges and new opportunities to restore the Jews in their homeland; we can see the emergence of the Jewish state as a providential sign of ongoing love. Our beloved God is knocking at the door; let us not allow this opportunity to pass us by due to our indifference or lethargy.

The theme of Rabbi Soloveitchik's address may be applied not only to the national love relationship of God and the people of Israel. It is also a very personal message to each individual.

It is possible to go through life without being attentive to God's "knocking on the door." We experience the wonders of nature; we are elevated by a glorious piece of music or art; we have a moment of spiritual epiphany; we heal from an illness; we recover from a crisis. These are moments when God is knocking at the door. Are we too tired or too busy or too spiritually numb to respond to the knocking? Do we let precious moments and incredible opportunities pass us by?

"Hark, my beloved knocks."

Shadow Lives

And maidens [*alamot*] without number.

(SONG OF SONGS 6:8)

The simple meaning of this phrase is that although the king has many wives and many women who admire him, his love is directed toward his special beloved maiden. The rabbis of the Midrash offered a deeper reading of this passage: "Do not read *alamot* [maidens] but read *olamot* [worlds]" (*Yalkut Shimoni*, Song of Songs, 247). According to this midrashic reading, the verse is teaching that there are limitless worlds. But what does that mean?

At the beginning of creation, the universe was chaos and void. It began in darkness and confusion, and these forces continue to pervade the world; our task is to bring light and order through our service to God. In the highest heights and deepest depths, there is divine light and holiness. There are countless "worlds"—dimensions of reality—that hover between total darkness and total light.[1]

Pushing this midrashic reading a bit further, the words *alamot/ olamot* are related to the word *ne'elam*, "hidden." There are countless hidden, unrevealed aspects to the universe—and to our lives.

Throughout our lifetimes, we have constantly made choices—what college to attend, what career to follow, whom to marry, where to live, what friends to have, what level of religious observance to keep. Indeed, everything we are today is the result of the numerous choices we have made throughout the years. We may look back at our various choices and ask: Were they right or wrong? Should I have done this or that? Am I living my true life? Have I actually taken a wrong path, a path not true to myself, to who I really am?

All of us live our lives, but we also are trailed by a plethora of shadow lives, lives that we might have lived if we had made different choices. Sometimes, a shadow life might be truer to our essence than the life we are currently living. Our shadow lives are hidden, without number.

It is fruitless to second-guess all of our choices. We cannot turn back the clock. We do not live in the shadows of what might have been; we live in the light of the present moment. An ongoing challenge is to clear our minds enough to understand the significance of each moment; to think through the choices we have made; to shed light on the road ahead of us.

We live in a noisy, busy world. We often find ourselves surrounded by people or plugged into our computers, smartphones, and other technological gadgets. Our minds and souls are filled with a seemingly unending flow of static. We rush along from day to day, from meeting to meeting, from task to task ... which of us has time to think quietly about our lives, let alone our shadow lives?

Rabbi Harold Kushner wrote about a group of tourists on a safari in Africa. They had hired several native porters to lead them and to carry their gear. After three days, the porters said they would need to stop in order to rest for one day. They explained that they were not physically tired but that "we have walked too far too fast and now we must wait for our souls to catch up to us."[2]

Does it sometimes seem that we walk too far and too fast, leaving our souls behind in the process? Doesn't it make sense for us to take regular, periodic rests so that we can allow our souls to catch up with our bodies? How can we bring light into the chaos of our world?

In his book *Original Wisdom*, Robert Wolff describes his lengthy stays in Malaysia, among the aboriginal Sng'oi people. This preindustrial, preagricultural group lives in a lush green jungle area, without cars or cell phones, clocks, or schedules. They have what Wolff calls "original wisdom," basic wisdom that is the heritage of all human beings. But whereas modern humans have become fragmented and competitive, the Sng'oi live in pristine simplicity; they feel themselves to be part of the "All-That-Is," an overarching unity that ties all creations into one extended community. Wolff reports how he gradually absorbed the wisdom of the Sng'oi:

> I had frequent flashes of what I then called *oneness*, that magical sense of being one with literally everything in creation. Each time I had the oneness experience, it became more natural, more a part of me—not something that I knew, but something I *am*.[3]

Wolff observes:

> We in the West know our world from seeing, hearing, and measuring what we assume to be a complex thing with many parts.... In other areas of the world people know from *experiencing* their world as a living, organic whole, where everything relates to everything and where we blend in as but another part of that whole. That experience is not seeing, or hearing, or measuring—it is a direct experiencing of all that we are.[4]

If we are to experience the fullness of life, we should love life's mysteries and its arts with the totality of our being. We should be intrigued by the countless dimensions and hidden unities. As we allow ourselves time to rest so that our souls can catch up with us, we will find the inner strength to move ourselves and our world further from darkness and closer to light.

The World of Chaos and the World of Order

Set me as a seal upon your heart, as a seal upon your arm; for love is strong as death, jealousy is cruel as the grave; the flashes thereof are flashes of fire, a very flame of the Lord. Many waters cannot quench love, neither can the floods drown it; if a man would give all the substance of his house for love, he would utterly be contemned.

(SONG OF SONGS 8:6–7)

Many waters cannot quench love, neither can the floods drown it. But true love does not entail negation of everyone and everything other than the beloved. Indeed, such a love becomes akin to self-love; it can become destructive.

In one of his essays, Rabbi Abraham Isaac Kook wrote that the "world of order" is based on propriety, good character, and conformity to law. "Every rebellion against this, whether inspired by levity or by the stirring of a higher spirit, reflects the world of chaos." Rabbi Kook noted that "the great idealists seek an order so noble, so firm and pure, beyond what may be found in the world of reality, and thus they destroy what has been fashioned in conformity to the norms of the world." While the best idealists know how to rebuild the world that has thus been destroyed, those of lesser stature are destroyers and "are rooted in the realm of chaos, on its lowest level." The souls of those who are inspired by the realm of chaos seek too much. "Their endless striving knows no bounds; they robe themselves in various forms, aspiring constantly to what is beyond the measure of the possible."[1]

188

It is possible to love God, to love perfection, too much! It is possible to foster a spiritual idealism that is so far removed from normal human life that it becomes destructive. Without realizing it, one might slip into the realm of chaos rather than remaining in the realm of order.

The Talmud (*Berakhot* 32b) relates that very pious people used to contemplate for an hour before they prayed; then they prayed; then they devoted another hour to meditation following their prayers. (The "hour" in this passage does not necessarily refer to a period of sixty minutes but more likely to an unspecified shorter amount of time in which these pious people could concentrate their thoughts.) The meditation before recitation of prayer was a means of attaining the proper mental and spiritual framework so that the prayer could be recited with appropriate *kavanah*, "intention." But what was the purpose of the meditation after the prayer had been completed?

Perhaps the lesson is, just as it requires special concentration to enter the holiness of communion with God, so it also requires concentration to return to regular, mundane life. After attaining a spiritual high, one needs to draw on that inspiration in order to be able to conduct earthly life imbued with that spirit. After prayer, one needs to "decompress," to come down from the lofty spiritual heights and reenter everyday life with an enhanced spiritual wakefulness.

We do not and cannot live on a perpetual spiritual high. A healthy spirituality seeks the lofty experience but is equally concerned with living sensibly, intelligently, and practically in our earthly home. Our love of God is not confined to those special moments of spiritual communion but is manifested in the way we live our lives every moment of every day.

Indeed, true love of God must inevitably find expression in true love of human beings who are created in the image of God. Spiritual life that is divorced from active involvement in the betterment of society is sterile and self-serving. The journalist and author David Brooks has stated it well:

We sometimes think of saints, or of people who are living like saints, as being ethereal, living in a higher spiritual realm. But often enough they live in an even less ethereal way than the rest of us. They are more fully of this earth, more fully engaged in the dirty, practical problems of the people around them.[2]

The "world of order" is more demanding—and more spiritual—than the "world of chaos." To ignore this truth is to bring the world closer to chaos.

Redemption

Make haste, my beloved, and be like a gazelle or a young hart upon the mountain of spices.

(SONG OF SONGS 8:14)

The Midrash interprets this verse as a prayer: "May You, God, hasten the redemption and cause Your presence to dwell on Mount Moriah [the site of the ancient Temples in Jerusalem]" (*Song of Songs Rabbah* 8:14). Thus, the Song of Songs, the love song of God and Israel, concludes with the hope for messianic redemption, a time when the people of Israel and all the nations of the world will live in peace, under the loving guidance of the Almighty.

The identification of "the mountain of spices" with Mount Moriah is significant. Mount Moriah is one of the two most important mountains in the Torah tradition, the other being Mount Sinai.

Mount Sinai was the site of the Revelation of God to the people of Israel. This was the place where the Torah was given, where Judaism was established. Yet, we do not actually know where Mount Sinai is! Some claim to identify this mountain, but we do not have a clear, unbroken tradition as to its real location. We don't have major tours and excursions to this holy place. We don't pray facing toward Mount Sinai.

Mount Moriah is identified in our tradition as the site of the "binding of Isaac" and as the place where Jacob had his wondrous dream in which he envisioned a great ladder connecting heaven and earth, with angels ascending and descending it. We know exactly where Mount Moriah is, and we visit it often. It is better known today as the Temple Mount, the place in Jerusalem where the ancient Temples stood and where the Western Wall remains as a reminder of the sanctity of the place. When we pray, we face toward Mount Moriah.

Why is Mount Sinai—the place of the ultimate Revelation of God to the Israelites—so insignificant as an ongoing religious site, whereas Mount Moriah has continued to be a central feature of our religious life over all the centuries?

In the case of Mount Sinai, the place of the Revelation is not the essential thing; the message is. The voice of God is everywhere and for all time and is not limited to a particular mountain. Rabbinic teaching has it that each day a divine voice calls out from Sinai, reminding us to study Torah and be loyal to its words. We do not know where Mount Sinai is because it is a symbol of every place. We do not have tours to Mount Sinai because the voice of God is everywhere.

Mount Moriah—the location of the binding of Isaac and of Jacob's dream—represents a different religious reality. If Mount Sinai symbolizes God speaking out to humans, Mount Moriah symbolizes frail human beings reaching out to God. Whereas the Revelation at Mount Sinai was witnessed by hundreds of thousands of Israelites, the binding of Isaac and Jacob's dream were experienced privately, without public fanfare. If the Torah had not recorded these stories, we would never have known about them. Mount Moriah gained its sanctity and centrality not as the place where God dramatically spoke out to humans, as at Sinai, but from the quiet, pious, sacrificial, and sturdy faith of lonely human beings crying out to God.

The site of the Temple Mount was sanctified by memories of the devotion, faith, and frailty of our ancestors. The Temple was where humans reached out to the Almighty, where they brought their first fruits in thanksgiving, where they brought sin offerings. The measure of the sacrificial service was determined by the sincerity of the people, by their joy or contrition—known only to themselves and to God. Mount Moriah is of eternal significance to us because it reflects our inner religious life and aspirations. It is symbolic of our reaching out to God in good times and bad.

Our tradition speaks of a third mountain: the Mountain of God. Psalm 24 asks, "Who shall ascend the Mountain of God, and who shall stand in His holy place?" It answers, "The clean of hands and pure of heart, who has not taken His name in vain nor sworn deceitfully" (Psalm 24:3–4).

We each climb our own mountain. Each of our lives is an attempt to ascend closer to God, closer to personal fulfillment. Some people climb mountains that seem wonderful and strong but are essentially hollow. Others climb mountains that seem quiet and unextraordinary, but they are strong and lasting. The measure of our success is not our wealth, fame, or popularity; the measure is being clean of hands, pure of heart, sanctifying God's name, being honest and trustworthy.

Mount Sinai reminds us that God speaks to us. Mount Moriah reminds us that we long for God. The Mountain of God reminds us that we have lives to lead, mountains to climb, things to accomplish. These three mountains together help us structure our lives and our religious imaginations.[1]

"I lift my eyes unto the mountains, whence comes my help? My help is from the Lord, Maker of heaven and earth" (Psalm 121:1–2).

Epilogue

In his short story "The Last Channel," Italo Calvino portrays a man who has been deemed to be insane. When he watched television, he kept clicking his remote control button without watching any program for more than a few seconds. At some point, he started to take the remote control panel outside his house. He clicked it at buildings, stores, banks, neon signs, and people.

But this man claimed that he was not at all deranged. In his defense, he stated that he kept clicking the remote control button because he did not like what he saw! He was looking for the "true" program, a program without drivel and artificiality and hypocrisy. He asserted, "There is an unknown station transmitting a story that has to do with me, *my* story, the only story that can explain to me who I am, where I come from and where I'm going."[1]

This man pushed the remote control button because he was looking for the "real" program, the "real" city, his "real" self. He wanted to turn off the chaos and senselessness around him and was certain that if he kept clicking the remote control button he would at last find the "right" channel.

While the man in Calvino's story seems to have crossed the line between sanity and insanity, his desire for self-understanding and for the perfection of the world are not insane at all. Don't we all wish we had a remote control button that we could click and make everything right, find the "real" picture, the "real" world that makes sense to us? When we confront lies and hatred, violence and injustice, hedonism and meanness—wouldn't it be nice to have a button to click to change the channel to a better picture?

In a sense, the biblical books ascribed to King Solomon can serve as remote control buttons. When we click onto these books, we can gain clarity about ourselves, about our society, about our relationship with God. We can come closer to finding the "story that has to do with me, *my* story, the only story that can explain to me who I am, where I come from, and where I'm going."

When we study Ecclesiastes, we explore our personal philosophy of life. Solomon's frustrations and doubts reflect our own perplexities and misgivings. Ecclesiastes comes to the following conclusion: Fear the Almighty, follow God's commandments, for this is the essence of a human being. See beyond the vanity of vanities of life; do not get depressed by the infinitesimal time and space of our lives. Each of us has something of the infinite within us. George Bernard Shaw, in an appreciation of Albert Einstein, wisely pointed out:

> Our lives are so small that we are too often in our solitude like children crying in the dark. Nevertheless our little solitude is a great and august solitude in which we can contemplate things that are greater than mankind.[2]

When we study Proverbs, we explore the basis for maintaining a healthy and happy society. In spite of the lies, cruelty, and ignorance that are so ubiquitous in our world, we have the power to click to another channel, to refocus on truth, compassion, and wisdom. We can demonstrate the moral courage to stand up against corruption and hypocrisy. We can join with like-minded idealists in helping to shape a humane and righteous society. With Solomon, we can arrive at the ultimate truth: "He who walks uprightly walks securely" (Proverbs 10:9).

When we study the Song of Songs, we explore our spiritual nature, our yearning for relationship with God. We click our remote control button to change the channel from a religiosity that is self-serving, superstitious, authoritarian, and obscurantist. We change the channel when we see those who speak in God's name while advocating murder, terrorism, hatred, and persecution. We keep clicking the remote control button until we arrive at a genuine, quiet, soul-satisfying intimacy with the Almighty. We keep clicking and searching until we can truly and tenderly say, as King Solomon said, "I am my Beloved's, and my Beloved is mine" (Song of Songs 6:3).

Acknowledgments

When I first discussed the idea of this book with Stuart Matlins of Jewish Lights, he immediately invited me to undertake the project. I thank him for his encouragement and wise guidance.

I am grateful to Stuart M. Matlins, publisher; Emily Wichland, vice president of Editorial and Production; Tim Holtz, director of Design and Production; Barbara Heise, vice president of Sales and Marketing; and Leah Brewer, publicist. It is always a pleasure to work with the staff of Jewish Lights, and I thank each of them for their roles in bringing this book to light.

I thank students in my Tuesday morning class "The Wisdom of Solomon," sponsored by the Institute for Jewish Ideas and Ideals (jewishideas.org). Their questions and insights have found their ways into this volume.

My beloved wife, Gilda, has read through the entire manuscript, offering her perceptive editorial advice. I thank her and our children, Rabbi Hayyim and Maxine Angel, Ronda Angel and Dr. Dan Arking, and Elana Angel and Dr. James Nussbaum; and our grandchildren, Jake Nussbaum, Andrew Arking, Jonathan Arking, Max Nussbaum, Charles Nussbaum, Jeremy Arking, Kara Nussbaum, Aviva Angel, Dahlia Angel, and Mordechai Pinchas Angel.

I thank the members and friends of the Institute for Jewish Ideas and Ideals for their friendship, loyalty, and support. Some of the material in this volume has been drawn from my weekly "Angel for Shabbat" column, published by the institute.

I thank the Almighty for having brought me to this special moment.

Notes

Introduction
1. Moshe Almosnino, *Yedei Moshe* (Tel Aviv: Hamachon leHeker Yahadut Saloniki, 1980).
2. Hayyim Angel, *Vision from the Prophet and Counsel from the Elders* (New York: Orthodox Union Press, 2013), 300.

Confronting Mortality
1. Amnon Shamosh, "The Great Confession," *Moment*, January 1983, 49.
2. Marc D. Angel, *The Orphaned Adult* (New York: Human Sciences Press, 1987).
3. Peter De Vries, *Let Me Count the Ways* (Boston: Little, Brown, 1965), 176.

Creativity and Wonder
1. Stephen Hawking, ed., *A Stubbornly Persistent Illusion: The Essential Scientific Work of Albert Einstein* (Philadelphia: Running Press, 2009), 342.
2. Ibid., 341–42.

Humility: The Root of Wisdom
1. Aryeh Kaplan, *Jewish Meditation* (New York: Schocken Books, 1985), 87.
2. Plato, *Plato*, trans. B. Jowett (Roslyn, NY: Walter J. Black, 1942), 39.

Imperfect Humanity
1. Isaiah Berlin, *The Proper Study of Mankind* (New York: Farrar, Straus and Giroux, 1997), 16.
2. Robert Winters, quoted by Sylvia Nasar, *A Beautiful Mind* (New York: Simon and Schuster, 1998), 304.

The Rat Race
1. Google UBS Wealth Management America, "UBS Investor Watch Report Examines What Drives Millionaires" (April 28, 2015): www.ubs.com/us/en/wealth/news/wealth-management-americas-news.html/en/2015/04/28/ubs-investor-watch-2015-2Q.html.
2. Harold Kushner, *When All You've Ever Wanted Isn't Enough* (New York: Simon and Schuster, 1987), 17.
3. Barry Schwartz, *The Paradox of Choice* (New York: HarperCollins, 2004), 221.
4. Alan Watts, *Psychotherapy East and West* (New York: Viking Press, 1974), 9.

Looking Forward
1. Marc D. Angel, *Angel for Shabbat*, vol. 1 (New York: Institute for Jewish Ideas and Ideals, 2010), 33–34. This comment, attributed to Rabbi Kook, has been passed down orally by his students.

Fame and Immortality
1. Sarah Kaplan, "American Exceptionalism and the 'Exceptionally American' Problem of Mass Shootings," *Washington Post* (August 27, 2015): www.

washingtonpost.com/news/morning-mix/wp/2015/08/27/american-exceptionalism-and-the-exceptionally-american-problem-of-mass-shootings/.

Humor and Happiness

1. Abraham Twerski, *Happiness and the Human Spirit* (Woodstock, VT: Jewish Lights, 2009), 73.
2. Ibid., 79.

A Time to Be Born and a Time to Die

1. Lewis Thomas, *The Lives of a Cell* (New York: Penguin, 1978), 58–59.
2. Oliver Sacks, "Sabbath," *New York Times* (August 16, 2015): www.nytimes.com/2015/08/16/opinion/sunday/oliver-sacks-sabbath.html?emc=eta1&_r=0.
3. Thornton Wilder, *Three Plays* (New York: Bantam Books, 1961), xi.

The Haves and Have-Nots

1. Cited by Richard Rubenstein, *The Age of Triage* (Boston: Beacon Press, 1983), 52.
2. Marc D. Angel, *Angel for Shabbat*, vol. 3 (New York: Institute for Jewish Ideas and Ideals, 2015), 57–58.

Essential Human Nature

1. Frans de Waal, *The Age of Empathy* (New York: Crown Archetype, 2010).
2. Michael McCullough, *Beyond Revenge* (San Francisco: Jossey-Bass, 2008).
3. Yitzhak Shemuel Reggio, *Commentary on Torah*, vol. 5 (Jerusalem: Y. S. Harary, 5764), 166.
4. This comment, attributed to Rabbi Soloveitchik, has been passed down orally by his students.

The March of Folly

1. Barbara Tuchman, *The March of Folly* (New York: Ballantine Books, 1984), 85.
2. Daniel Kahneman, *Thinking Fast and Slow* (New York: Farrar, Straus and Giroux, 2013).

Rich but Unsatisfied

1. David Myers, *The American Paradox: Spiritual Hunger in an Age of Plenty* (New Haven: Yale University Press, 2000), cited in Barry Schwartz, *The Paradox of Choice* (New York: HarperCollins, 2004), 109.

Life Isn't Always Fair

1. Inda Schaenen, *Speaking of Fourth Grade* (New York: New Press, 2014), 31.

Tablets: Shattered and Whole

1. Marc D. Angel, *Angel for Shabbat*, vol. 1 (New York: Institute for Jewish Ideas and Ideals, 2010), 68–69.

Being Natural, Not Pretentious

1. Alan Watts, *The Supreme Identity* (New York: Knopf, 1972), 128.
2. Marc D. Angel, trans., *The Essential Pele Yoetz* (New York: Sepher-Hermon Press, 1991), 116.
3. Marc D. Angel, *Angel for Shabbat*, vol. 3 (New York: Institute for Jewish Ideas and Ideals, 2015), 225–26.

Goodness and Ingratitude
1. Marc D. Angel, *Angel for Shabbat*, vol. 3 (New York: Institute for Jewish Ideas and Ideals, 2015), 102–3.

When There Is Life—Live!
1. Brendan Gill, *Late Bloomers* (New York: Artisan, 1998).
2. Abraham Twerski, *Happiness and the Human Spirit* (Woodstock, VT: Jewish Lights, 2009), 91.

Koheleth's Ultimate Insights
1. Gail Sheehy, *Passages* (New York: E. P. Dutton, 1974), 6.
2. Ibid., 8.
3. Harold Kushner, *When All You've Ever Wanted Isn't Enough* (New York: Simon and Schuster, 1987), 140–41.

The Wisdom of Our Fathers and Our Mothers
1. Joseph B. Soloveitchik, *The Lonely Man of Faith* (New York: Doubleday, 1992), 47.
2. Joseph B. Soloveitchik, "A Tribute to the Rebbetzin of Talne," *Tradition* 17, no. 2 (1978): 77.

We Are Caretakers, Not Owners
1. Marc D. Angel, *Angel for Shabbat*, vol. 2 (New York: Institute for Jewish Ideas and Ideals, 2013), 200–1.

Resilience When Facing Adversity
1. Dee Wedemeyer, "His Life Is His Mind," *New York Times Magazine* (August 18, 1996): www.nytimes.com/1996/08/18/magazine/his-life-is-his-mind.html?pagewanted=all.
2. Ibid.
3. Mandy Oaklander, "Bounce Back," *Time* (June 1, 2015): http://time.com/3892044/the-science-of-bouncing-back.
4. Adin Steinsaltz, *Talks on the Parasha* (Jerusalem: Maggid Books, 2015), 48.

Religion at Its Best ... and Worst
1. Alexandr Solzhenitsyn, *The Gulag Archipelago* (New York: Harper and Row, 1973), 168.
2. Adam Grant, "Raising a Moral Child," *New York Times* (April 13, 2014): www.nytimes.com/2014/04/12/opinion/sunday/raising-a-moral-child.html?_r=0.
3. Marc D. Angel, *Angel for Shabbat*, vol. 3 (New York: Institute for Jewish Ideas and Ideals, 2015), 143–44.

What Do We Remember about the Righteous?
1. Atul Gawande, *Being Mortal* (New York: Henry Holt, 2014), 126–27.
2. Ibid.

No Secrets from God
1. Arthur Miller, *Collected Plays* (New York: Viking Press, 1957), 115.
2. David McCullough, *Truman* (New York: Simon and Schuster, 1992), 272ff.

When We Are Betrayed

1. Marc D. Angel, *Angel for Shabbat*, vol. 3 (New York: Institute for Jewish Ideas and Ideals, 2015), 118–19.

What Is Humility?

1. This topic is discussed in Eliezer Berkovits, *Faith after the Holocaust* (New York: Ktav, 1977).

The Individual and Society

1. Elias Canetti, *Crowds and Power* (New York: Seabury Press, 1978).

Transmitting Culture from Generation to Generation

1. Margaret Mead, *Culture and Commitment* (Garden City, NY: Natural History Press, 1970).
2. Sherry Turkle, *Reclaiming Conversation: The Power of Talk in a Digital Age* (New York: Penguin Press, 2015).

Understanding Oneself ... and Others

1. Martin Buber, *I and Thou* (New York: Charles Scribner's Sons, 1970).

Role Models—Positive and Negative

1. Rene Girard, *Mimesis and Theory* (Stanford, CA: Stanford University Press, 2008), 78.

Developing the "Self"

1. Marc D. Angel, *Losing the Rat Race, Winning at Life* (Jerusalem: Urim Publications, 2005), 73.
2. Ralph Waldo Emerson, *Essays, Poems, Addresses* (Roslyn, NY: Walter J. Black, 1941), 120.

Grandparents and Grandchildren

1. Joseph B. Soloveitchik, *Man of Faith in the Modern World*, ed. Abraham Besdin (Hoboken, NJ: Ktav, 1989), 15.

The Generation of the Lie

1. Martin Buber, *Good and Evil* (New York: Charles Scribner's Sons, 1952), 10.
2. Albert Einstein, *Out of My Later Years* (Secaucus, NJ: Citadel Press, 1956), 10.

The Dignity of Growing Old

1. Atul Gawande, *Being Mortal* (New York: Henry Holt, 2014), 18.

When People Disappoint You

1. Adin Steinsaltz, *Talks on the Parasha* (Jerusalem: Maggid Books, 2015), 313.
2. Yitzchak Breitowitz, "When Leaders Fail: Healing from Rabbinic Scandal," *Jewish Action* (Summer 2015): www.ou.org/jewish_action/06/2015/when-leaders-fail-healing-from-rabbinic-scandal.

Standing Up to Bullies

1. Yeshaya Leibowitz, *Accepting the Yoke of Heaven* (Jerusalem: Urim Publications, 2002).
2. Michael McCullough, *Beyond Revenge* (San Francisco: Jossey-Bass, 2008), 35.

Egomaniacs and Their Masks

1. Christine Porath, "No Time to Be at Work," *New York Times* (June 21, 2015): www.nytimes.com/2015/06/21/opinion/sunday/is-your-boss-mean.html?mwrsm=email.
2. Ibid.
3. Elias Canetti, *Crowds and Power* (New York: Seabury Press, 1978), 377.

Deveikut–Clinging to God

1. Moshe Almosnino, *Yedei Moshe* (Tel Aviv: Hamachon leHeker Yahadut Saloniki, 1980), 25.
2. Aryeh Kaplan, *Jewish Meditation* (New York: Schocken Books, 1985), 112.

Maintaining Spiritual Balance

1. Shlomo Aviner, *Ta'alumot* (Jerusalem: Yeshivat Ateret Yerushalayim, 2015), 190.

Looking after Our Spiritual Needs

1. Marc D. Angel, *Commentary on Pirkei Avot* (Jerusalem: Koren Publishers, 2015), 4.
2. Erich Fromm, *The Heart of Man* (New York: Harper and Row, 1964), 138.

Think Carefully, Avoid the Charlatans

1. Franz Kafka, *The Castle* (New York: Schocken Books, 1974), 63.
2. Moshe Almosnino, *Yedei Moshe* (Tel Aviv: Hamachon leHeker Yahadut Saloniki, 1980), 33–34.

Authenticity

1. Abraham Joshua Heschel, in the proceedings of the Rabbinical Assembly of America, 53rd Annual Convention, Atlantic City, New Jersey, 1953, 152: www.rabbinicalassembly.org/sites/default/files/public/resources-ideas/cj/classics/9-7-11-b2school/heschel-1953.pdf.
2. Marc D. Angel, *Angel for Shabbat*, vol. 3 (New York: Institute for Jewish Ideas and Ideals, 2015), 145–46.

The Courage to Stand Alone

1. Joseph B. Soloveitchik, *The Lonely Man of Faith* (New York: Doubleday, 1992).

Love of God

1. Moshe Almosnino, *Yedei Moshe* (Tel Aviv: Hamachon leHeker Yahadut Saloniki, 1980), 53.
2. Adin Steinsaltz, *Talks on the Parasha* (Jerusalem: Maggid Books, 2015), 30.

The Yearnings of Love

1. David Brooks, *The Road to Character* (New York: Random House, 2015), 174.
2. Abraham Isaac Kook, *The Lights of Penitence, The Moral Principles, Essays, Letters, and Poems*, trans. and ed. Ben Zion Bokser (New York: Paulist Press, 1978), 379.

Truth and Compassion

1. Marc D. Angel, *Angel for Shabbat*, vol. 1 (New York: Institute for Jewish Ideas and Ideals, 2010), 158–59.

Setting God Before Us at All Times
1. Harold Kushner, *Overcoming Life's Disappointments* (New York: Anchor Books, 2006), 27–28.

Spiritual Spoilers
1. Marc D. Angel, *Maimonides, Spinoza and Us: Toward an Intellectually Vibrant Judaism* (Woodstock, VT: Jewish Lights, 2009), chapter 6.

Hitbodedut—Meditation
1. Leonard Mlodinow, *The Upright Thinkers* (New York: Pantheon Books, 2015).
2. Aryeh Kaplan, *Meditation and Kabbalah* (York Beach, ME: Samuel Weiser, 1982), 310.
3. Ibid.

Shalom—In Search of Wholeness
1. Ovadia Seforno on Numbers 6:25.

God's Name Is Truth
1. Moshe Almosnino, *Yedei Moshe* (Tel Aviv: Hamachon leHeker Yahadut Saloniki, 1980), 81.
2. George Orwell, *1984* (New York: Signet Classic, 1977), 4.
3. *Krulewitch v. United States*, 336 U.S. 440, 458 (1949), Jackson concurring.
4. Marc D. Angel, *Angel for Shabbat*, vol. 2 (New York: Institute for Jewish Ideas and Ideals, 2013), 110–11.

Being Awake to New Challenges
1. Joseph B. Soloveitchik, *Besod haYahad ve-haYahid*, ed. Pinchas Peli (Jerusalem: Orot Publishers, 1976), 331–400.

Shadow Lives
1. Shlomo Aviner, *Ta'alumot* (Jerusalem: Yeshivat Ateret Yerushalayim, 2015), 83.
2. Harold Kushner, *The Lord Is My Shepherd* (New York: Anchor Books, 2004), 60.
3. Robert Wolff, *Original Wisdom* (Rochester, VT: Inner Traditions, 2001), 164.
4. Ibid., 193.

The World of Chaos and the World of Order
1. Abraham Isaac Kook, *The Lights of Penitence, The Moral Principles, Essays, Letters, and Poems*, trans. and ed. Ben Zion Bokser (New York: Paulist Press, 1978), 256.
2. David Brooks, *The Road to Character* (New York: Random House, 2015), 91.

Redemption
1. Marc D. Angel, *Angel for Shabbat*, vol. 2 (New York: Institute for Jewish Ideas and Ideals, 2013), 29–30.

Epilogue
1. Italo Calvino, *Numbers in the Dark* (New York: Vintage Books, 1996), 256.
2. Albert Einstein, *Einstein on Cosmic Religion and Other Opinions and Aphorisms* (Mineola, NY: Dover Publications, 2009), 39.

Suggestions for Further Reading

Almosnino, Moshe. *Yedei Moshe*. Tel Aviv: Hamachon leHeker Yahadut Saloniki, 5740 (1980).

Angel, Hayyim. *Vision from the Prophet and Counsel from the Elders*. New York: Orthodox Union Press, 2013.

Angel, Marc D. *Angel for Shabbat*. Vol. 1. New York: Institute for Jewish Ideas and Ideals, 2010.

———. *Angel for Shabbat*. Vol. 2. New York: Institute for Jewish Ideas and Ideals, 2013.

———. *Angel for Shabbat*. Vol. 3. New York: Institute for Jewish Ideas and Ideals, 2015.

———. *Commentary on Pirkei Avot*. Jerusalem: Koren Publishers, 2015.

———. *Foundations of Sephardic Spirituality: The Inner Life of Jews of the Ottoman Empire*. Woodstock, VT: Jewish Lights, 2006.

———. *Losing the Rat Race, Winning at Life*. Jerusalem: Urim Publications, 2005.

———. *Maimonides: Essential Teachings on Jewish Faith and Ethics*. Woodstock, VT: Jewish Lights, 2012.

———. *Maimonides, Spinoza and Us: Toward an Intellectually Vibrant Judaism*. Woodstock, VT: Jewish Lights, 2009.

———. *The Orphaned Adult*. New York: Human Sciences Press, 1987.

———. *The Rhythms of Jewish Living: A Sephardic Exploration of Judaism's Spirituality*. Woodstock, VT: Jewish Lights, 2015.

Aviner, Shlomo. *Ta'alumot*. Jerusalem: Yeshivat Ateret Yerushalayim, 5775 (2015).

Berger, Peter, and Kellner, H. *The Homeless Mind*. New York: Random House, 1973.

Berlin, Isaiah. *The Proper Study of Mankind*. New York: Farrar, Straus and Giroux, 1997.

Brooks, David. *The Road to Character*. New York: Random House, 2015.

Buber, Martin. *Good and Evil*. New York: Charles Scribner's Sons, 1952.

———. *I and Thou*. New York: Charles Scribner's Sons, 1970.

Canetti, Elias. *Crowds and Power*. New York: Seabury Press, 1978.

Cohen, A., ed. and trans. *The Five Megilloth*. London: Soncino Press, 1967.

———. *Proverbs*. London: Soncino Press, 1967.

De Waal, Frans. *The Age of Empathy*. New York: Crown Archetype, 2010.

Einstein, Albert. *Einstein on Cosmic Religion and Other Opinions and Aphorisms*. Mineola, NY: Dover Publications, 2009.

———. *Out of My Later Years*. Secaucus, NJ: Citadel Press, 1956.

Frankl, Viktor. *Man's Search for Meaning*. New York: Washington Square Press, 1984.

Fromm, Erich. *The Heart of Man*. New York: Harper and Row, 1964.

Gawande, Atul. *Being Mortal*. New York: Henry Holt, 2014.

Girard, Rene. *Mimesis and Theory*. Stanford, CA: Stanford University Press, 2008.

Kahneman, Daniel. *Thinking Fast and Slow*. New York: Farrar, Straus and Giroux, 2013.

Kaplan, Aryeh. *Jewish Meditation*. New York: Schocken Books, 1985.

———. *Meditation and Kabbalah*. York Beach, ME: Samuel Weiser, 1982.

Kook, Abraham Isaac. *The Lights of Penitence, The Moral Principles, Essays, Letters, and Poems*. Translated and edited by Ben Zion Bokser. New York: Paulist Press, 1978.

Kushner, Harold. *Living a Life That Matters*. New York: Anchor Books, 2001.

———. *Overcoming Life's Disappointments*. New York: Anchor Books, 2006.

———. *The Lord Is My Shepherd*. New York: Anchor Books, 2004.

———. *When All You've Ever Wanted Isn't Enough*. New York: Simon and Schuster, 1987.

Lau, Binyamin. *The Sages*. Vol. 4. Jerusalem: Maggid Books, 2015.

Leibowitz, Yeshaya. *Accepting the Yoke of Heaven*. Jerusalem: Urim Publications, 2002.

McCullough, David. *Truman*. New York: Simon and Schuster, 1992.

McCullough, Michael. *Beyond Revenge*. San Francisco: Jossey-Bass, 2008.

Mead, Margaret. *Culture and Commitment*. Garden City, NY: Natural History Press, 1970.

Miller, Arthur. *Collected Plays*. New York: Viking Press, 1957.

Mlodinow, Leonard. *The Upright Thinkers*. New York: Pantheon Books, 2015.

Myers, David. *The American Paradox: Spiritual Hunger in an Age of Plenty*. New Haven: Yale University Press, 2000.

Schaenen, Inda. *Speaking of Fourth Grade*. New York: New Press, 2014.

Schwartz, Barry. *The Paradox of Choice*. New York: HarperCollins, 2004.

Sheehy, Gail. *Passages*. New York: E. P. Dutton, 1974.

Soloveitchik, Joseph B. "A Tribute to the Rebbetzin of Talne." *Tradition* 17, no. 2 (1978): 73–83.

———. *BeSod haYahid veHaYahad*. Edited by Pinchas Peli. Jerusalem: Orot, 5736 (1976).

———. *The Lonely Man of Faith*. New York: Doubleday, 1992.

Solzhenitsyn, Alexandr. *The Gulag Archipelago*. New York: Harper and Row, 1973.

Steinsaltz, Adin. *Talks on the Parasha*. Jerusalem: Maggid Books, 2015.

Thomas, Lewis. *The Lives of a Cell*. New York: Penguin, 1978.

Tuchman, Barbara. *The March of Folly*. New York: Ballantine Books, 1984.

Turkle, Sherry. *Reclaiming Conversation: The Power of Talk in a Digital Age*. New York: Penguin Publishing Group, 2015.

Twerski, Abraham. *Happiness and the Human Spirit*. Woodstock, VT: Jewish Lights, 2009.

Watts, Alan. *Psychotherapy East and West*. New York: Viking Press, 1974.

———. *The Supreme Identity*. New York: Knopf, 1972.

Wilder, Thornton. *Three Plays*. New York: Bantam Books, 1961.

Wolff, Robert. *Original Wisdom*. Rochester, VT: Inner Traditions, 2001.

www.ingramcontent.com/pod-product-compliance
Lightning Source LLC
Chambersburg PA
CBHW030506100426
42813CB00002B/357